POP GOES THE
CHURCH

WHAT OTHERS ARE SAYING ABOUT POP GOES THE CHURCH

"In thirty years of ministry, I have never stopped believing that the local church is the hope of the world. It is my driving passion to help leaders get this and to help them find tools to do church more effectively. *Pop Goes the Church* should be read by every pastor, church leader, and layperson who wants to connect people to Jesus but is finding it hard to be heard in our media-saturated culture.

Some authors have suggested we should give up on the local church. Stevens, however, is making the case that a local church can be transformational in its community. He doesn't stop with theory but gives practical how-tos and examples from churches of all sizes and styles.

Pop Goes the Church is sure to become very useful for a new generation of leaders. It will compel animated conversations in conference rooms and living rooms across the world as leaders everywhere wrestle with how to leverage pop culture in and through the local church."

—BILL HYBELS
Senior Pastor, Willow Creek Community Church
Chairman of the Board, Willow Creek Association

"Most companies, and probably churches, rearrange deckchairs on the Titanic. *Contemporary* doesn't equal *revolutionary*, and big, hairy, revolutionary change is what's needed for churches to survive and thrive. *Pop Goes the Church* provides a curve-jumping, revolution-starting approach to changing churches, so read it and make the world a better place."

—GUY KAWASAKI
Managing Director, Garage Technology Ventures
Author, *Art of the Start*

"I don't know a church in America that is better at using culture to engage people with God's truth than Granger Community Church. Tim Stevens' *Pop Goes the Church* will challenge you, convict you, and inspire you to be more intentional about doing whatever it takes to reach people with the message of Christ.

As a new believer in college, I'll never forget the Sunday I convinced four of my non-Christian fraternity brothers to visit church with me. Instead of meeting God, they were bored, disinterested, and confused. Too many churches understand God's Word, but don't know how to present it in a way that grabs attention and makes a difference. Tim Stevens' *Pop Goes the Church* destroys the myth that culturally relevant churches are always biblically shallow. This book inspires with unapologetic passion the mandate to present God's Word—but to do it in a way that connects with a spiritually apathetic world.

Tim Stevens and Granger Community Church have always inspired me. Their passion to communicate uncompromised biblical truth with cutting edge relevancy is second to none. This heartfelt call bleeds through each page of *Pop Goes the Church*. Stevens writes with a sense of urgency that will inspire your ministry to an authentic and relevant presentation of God's transforming Word."

—CRAIG GROESCHEL
Senior Pastor, LifeChurch.tv
Author, *Going All the Way*

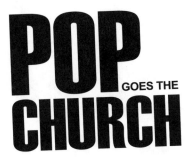

POP GOES THE CHURCH

SHOULD THE CHURCH ENGAGE POP CULTURE?

Tim Stevens

Indianapolis, Indiana

POP GOES THE CHURCH
Tim Stevens

ISBN-13: 978-0-9790174-9-0
ISBN-10: 0-9790174-9-1

Library of Congress Control Number: 2008922632

Power Publishing
5641 West 73rd Street
Indianapolis, IN 46278
(317) 347-1051
www.powerpublishinginc.com

This book is manufactured in the United States of America.

Editor: Susan Andres
Cover Design: Dustin Maust
Interior Design: Lisa DeSelm

Books by Tim Stevens:
Simply Strategic Growth: Attracting a Crowd to Your Church
Simply Strategic Volunteers: Empowering People for Ministry
Simply Strategic Stuff: Help for Leaders Drowning in the Details of Running a Church

ACKNOWLEDGEMENTS

My Wife She is the woman who still makes my heart beat fast every time she walks in the room (which makes it hard to write a book at home!). Faith has given me the space these past few months to labor over this book because of her commitment to our ministry together.

My Pastor Yes, I am a pastor, but I also *have* a pastor. Mark Beeson has been my friend, co-worker, boss, and pastor for more than thirteen years and graciously allowed me the time to work on this project. He believes in it as much as I do, and he has cheered me on all along the way.

My Church From the day I arrived, when three hundred people were gathering in a movie theater, to now when thousands are taking steps toward Christ—the people of Granger Community Church have always amazed me. They are in love with Jesus, quick to change, innovative, and passionate about leveraging the culture. There is no place I'd rather be.

My Team Writing a book is full time. Yet my day job did not go away. I am so thankful to my team who filled in the gaps and exceeded my expectations because of their passion to see this book finished. They include Georgia Fawcett, Dave Moore, Kem Meyer, Mark Waltz, Melanie Rosander, Jami Ruth, Rob Wegner, Butch Whitmire, and the rest of the team at Granger.

My Sidekicks With hundreds of e-mails, thousands of photocopies, and hours of research, I couldn't have finished *Pop Goes the Church* without the assistance of Adam Tarwacki and Theresa Hoeft. They each have a passion for excellence and willingness to serve that is unmatched.

My Publishers When I first decided to work with Tad Long and George Watkins, I knew I was taking a risk. Power Publishing is a small company with a short history. But it may prove to be one of the best risks I have ever taken. Their creativity in the process, flexibility in the design, partnership in the project, and long-term investment in the book's success has amazed me every step of the way.

NOTE TO READERS

⌨ KEYWORDS

Throughout *Pop Goes the Church* you will see this ⌨ computer screen symbol. Each time you see it, you will also find a keyword link to the book's companion website, PopGoesTheChurch.com. Enter the keyword on the website, and you will find videos, graphics, and additional stories connected with that keyword. The website also contains a blog that will include up-to-date examples of churches leveraging the culture, so check back often. See page 240 for a complete list of keyword references in this book.

CONTENTS

FOREWORD

After reading Tim's book, every Christian, especially every Christian leader, should respond with both frustration and excitement. The frustration stems from the stark reality that many churches are still far behind the curve in connecting with today's culture, let alone preparing for the ever-changing challenges we will face in the future. Excitement, though, should trump that frustration as we see that there is hope for the local church. As Tim so accurately and passionately points out, we as a church can become a difference maker in our communities. We can be relevant in meeting the real needs of real people. We can stay on the cutting edge of cultural trends, in the arts, music, and social needs.

When I started Fellowship Church with a small group of committed believers seventeen years ago, we began it with one simple credo—to bring the never-changing truth of the Gospel to an ever-changing culture in creative and compelling ways. I sensed a call to the ministry while playing basketball at Florida State University. And I wanted a church where even my unchurched college teammates would feel comfortable and find something relevant for their lives. I wanted them to connect with Christ right where they were. After all, that's what Christ did.

It is said of Jesus that he was a friend of sinners. That doesn't mean he tolerated them. That doesn't mean he took them on as an evangelistic project. It doesn't even mean he hung out with them out of pity. It means what it says. He was their friend. He cared about their needs, listened to their problems, and helped them in whatever situation to understand that God loved them—Jesus loved them. In fact, I might be making a stretch here (but I don't think so) in saying that he might have preferred hanging out with the sinners because there was no pretense or religious hypocrisy. His harshest criticism was not for the sinners but for the religious leaders of the day. He saw their rituals and legalism as oppressive, hypocritical, and extremely opposed to the spirit of the law. The law had become god and God had become (or seemed) irrelevant. Sound familiar? The law was meant to drive people into the loving embrace of the Father, not away from him.

Tim is so right. We do not worship the church; we worship God. The local church is the vehicle Christ left us to communicate and share our love for God. When the traditions of the church become supreme, God will seem very irrelevant to people, both inside and outside the walls of the church. As I've often said, the tendency of any church is to always look inward and become navel gazers. And when we bend over into our holy huddle, guess what the rest of the world sees. You got it! If we do not look outward intentionally and strategically to engage and become change agents in our culture, we will become self-obsessed and wrapped up in meaningless tradition. That is neither attractive nor helpful for a world looking for real answers to the real problems it faces in this new millennium.

As a church, we must answer Tim's questions in this book with all the honesty and guts we can muster: Would it make a difference in your community if your church simply ceased to exist? Would anyone even notice? That's a sobering thought, isn't it? I pray that churches and church leaders all over this country will take heed of the insight and foresight in this great book. We as a church cannot become irrelevant or all hope is lost. We must not only get up to speed in meeting the needs of our current culture but also lead the way into the future. For some reason, the church is always a few steps behind. Church leaders, let's change that trend together.

I must say that, while many churches are missing it, many are starting to get it right. I do see a new guard of forward thinking leaders who are heaven-bent on making a real difference in their communities. I see a resurgence of vision among many pastors in making the church a vital part of our complex global community. I see a passion to stay in touch with the arts, movies, the Internet, music and other cultural influences, so that we can leverage those in reaching people where they are.

Leaders, let's make the church exciting again. Let's keep it relevant. Let's start answering the questions that people are asking. And, yes, let's make it entertaining, because that simply means to capture and hold someone's attention. We can do that. We must do that. Christ was not boring or irrelevant. Shame on us if we make his church that way. This book is a great start in both diagnosing what's wrong and in providing solid answers and encouragement to fix it. Take this book to heart and begin to take the worthwhile journey toward creating a church of which Christ himself would be proud. For the sake of Christ and his kingdom, we are compelled to do nothing less.

—ED YOUNG
Senior Pastor, Fellowship Church
Author, *The Creative Leader*

INTRODUCTION

November 19, 1983 started out like any other day. It was a Saturday and I was a junior in high school, so I was looking for things to do and friends with whom to hang out. I had made plans to get together with my friend David Whiting. I don't recall what we were going to do, but I do remember that my parents had instructed me not to leave the house until I had finished my chores. No one else was home—just me, in my parents' bedroom vacuuming the carpet, and David, who was waiting for me in the living room.

Then it happened.

A huge explosion. Not like a firecracker that you hear outside your window on a summer night—not like gunfire that surprises you—not even like a loud clap of thunder during a spring storm. This was more like a concussion so strongly felt that it instantly messes up all your senses. This explosion was so powerful it literally picked me up off my feet and threw me across the floor.

My first thought: "Am I alive?" Even now, I get chills remembering the fear I felt in that moment.

My second thought was "What did David do?" I was positive the side of our house had just been blown apart and I could not imagine what David had done to cause it or the trouble I would be in because he did.

I ran down the hallway, stepping over the pictures that just seconds ago were hanging on the wall and now lay in disarray on the floor. In the kitchen, cups and silverware that had previously been on the countertop were now scattered across the floor.

I quickly found David. I could tell by the look on his face that he had no idea what had happened. We were both incredibly scared.

Let me define "scared." This wasn't the *I-just-scratched-dad's-car-and-I-have-to-tell-him* type of scared. Nor was it the *I'm-walking-home-at-night-*

and-I-just-heard-a-noise-in-the-bushes kind of scared. I've experienced fear at that level, and as bad as it is, this was much worse.

We were terrified. We had just experienced an explosion that was strong enough to knock us off our feet. To put it in perspective, you must remember the Cold War had not ended yet, and the talk of a nuclear strike from the Soviet Union was on the nightly news. We were the *freaked-out-physically-shaking-heart-beating-out-of-your-chest-can't-speak* version of scared.

We ran outside through the front door and noticed we were not alone. There were scores of people pouring out of their homes, standing around, gazing, talking, wondering aloud, and then eventually pointing to the east.

That is when I saw it: the biggest, billowing plume of black smoke I could ever imagine. It was exactly the mushroom-shaped image that follows a nuclear strike, which we had seen repeatedly on the evening news. I was certain we had been bombed. It didn't cross

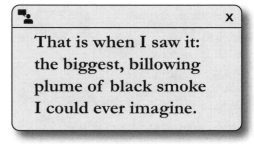

That is when I saw it: the biggest, billowing plume of black smoke I could ever imagine.

my mind to wonder why the Soviet Union would choose to strike Pleasant Hill, Iowa, on their initial assault. But it was undeniable, or so I thought.

In the days to come, the truth of the explosion came out. Back in the 1930s before World War II, a bunker had been built to hold military munitions. After the war, contractors used it to store dynamite for excavating and construction-clearing projects. As the city began to grow around it and subdivisions were constructed, the 25,000 pounds of dynamite stored there were to be removed from our community. This was scheduled to happen the following week.

The bunker was well built and heavily padlocked, and it had walls all the way around that were four bricks thick in order to protect it from hunters or vandals. Unfortunately, on that brisk fall day in 1983, two young boys had gone out target shooting. Clint Woodard, a ninth-grade student, and Jeffrey Waddell, his eighth-grade buddy, were not new to guns. They hunted together quite often. However, this time they became curious about the small block building with no windows and proceeded to climb on top of it. The best guess of the investigators is that they shot their guns down through the air vents on top of the bunker.

What resulted was an explosion in central Iowa that was also felt in the surrounding states of Nebraska, Minnesota, Missouri, and Illinois. Twenty-five homes in the area were blown completely off their foundations, causing millions of dollars in damage. Acres of trees in a one-mile radius all went up about eight or ten feet, then bent over away from the blast site at a ninety-degree angle. The resulting hole in the ground was seventy-five feet deep and one hundred feet across. No remains of the boys were ever found.*

What I will never forget about that day was the intensity of the impact. It still is so hard to comprehend that an explosion that was more than two miles away from my house could have blown me off my feet. And an event that only lasted a few seconds still lingers in my memory and pulls on my emotions twenty-five years later.

The events of that November day in 1983 had a huge impact. Not only on me, but on others in close proximity who also experienced the blast, on those who sustained property damage, and on the community as it wrestled with the danger of the leftover munitions. More than anyone, however, the family members of Clint Woodard and Jeffrey Waddell still feel the impact of that fateful day.

* A big thanks to Karen Stevens (yes, my mom) for researching this story. The facts are from several articles printed in the *Des Moines Register*, November 20–30, 1983.

An *impact* is defined as "the power of making a strong, immediate impression."[1] Every year, there are events happening locally, nationally, or globally that make a strong and immediate impression. In recent years, events of impact include Hurricane Katrina, the war in Iraq, the 2004 tsunami, and the terrorist attacks on 9/11. Locally, we experience events of significant influence when a company leaves town and hundreds of jobs are lost, or a flood wreaks havoc on a region.

Some events have a positive impact. For example, a new official might be elected and bring tax relief to a community. Or a new factory might open in a troubled community and employ hundreds of new people, causing an economic boom. A thriving college campus can have a very positive impact on a town.

But where are the churches that are making a *strong, immediate impression?* Where is the church that has an impact so significant it can't be denied by the community? Where is the church known more by what they *do* than by what they *say?* Where is the church whose members do not hesitate to invite their *unchurched* neighbors because they know the neighbors will be significantly influenced—their lives will never be the same? Where is the church that is offering weekend services about which the entire community is talking?

Would your community be any different if your church disappeared tomorrow? Have you ever asked yourself this question? Have you ever considered it with others at your church? If your church suddenly disappeared, could the community even recover? Or would they go on as though nothing at all had changed?

What is happening at your church that is worth talking about? When people leave your service, are they thinking about the e-mails they need to send and the football game they want to watch—or are they thinking deeply about their own choices and thinking how they might make a difference in someone's life this week? How is your church helping the people of the community? How is it helping the *down-and-outers* deal with poverty? How is it helping the *up-and-outers* deal with the pressures of money and health and busyness? How is your church helping solve the educational or crime issues in your community? How is your church helping people in the community to become better parents, have better marriages, make better decisions, become rooted in solid values and morals, or become better citizens and neighbors? How is your church helping people connect to Jesus?

I ask again, would your community be any different if your church ceased to exist? I don't only mean to you and your friends and others who already attend. I'm also talking about those who drive by your church and have never been inside. Would they feel a difference in the community because your church no longer existed?

Sadly, for most of us, the answer is a resounding "no." We didn't even have to think that long about the answer. Our church is great for our friends, our family, and us, but there is little measurable impact on the community. There is little happening that is making a difference outside of the few dozen or couple hundred who regularly attend.

Truthfully, most Christians would never think of inviting an unchurched person to their church. Just the thought of Joe (the guy who coaches the kids basketball team with you) coming to your church service makes you shudder. He wouldn't get it. Joe would make fun of the music. He wouldn't understand when is the right time to sit down or stand up. It would not make sense to Joe why you sit for an hour and listen to a guy who is boring talk about the Ark of the Covenant and the dimensions of the tabernacle. If Joe came to your church, you would never hear the end of it.

And so our world is filled with impotent churches. Nothing is happening. A few people attend, someone mows the lawn, and the pastor visits people in the hospital, but when you look for the impact

Dear Joe,

As I was writing about you, it crossed my mind that you might actually be reading this book. Even though you are fed up with churches and church people, that doesn't mean you aren't a spiritual being. In fact, it might tick you off a little bit that people think you aren't spiritual just because you don't go to church. You may feel judged by the very people who claim to follow Jesus.

For that, I'm sorry. May I suggest to you that we mean well? Most church people don't have bad intentions. They just don't know any better. They have been in the church bubble for so long that they have lost effectiveness in the real world without even knowing it. That is why I'm writing this book. I am hoping for a big outcome. I'd like to see a church in your community (and in every city) where you would be comfortable and not feel weird or be convinced that everyone else is weird and where the message actually made sense. In this church, there would be encouragement to engage your faith in the real world rather than a mandate to withdraw from the world in a sheltered, communal setting.

I realize that is a big dream, but hang with me. If you don't mind, I'd like to continue this dialogue with you through the rest of this book. I think there is a lot we can learn from each other.

-Tim

on the community around them—you see nothing. People like Joe begin to draw conclusions that the local church is dead. It is a place you attend out of duty, but when it comes to impact and making a difference, you expect nothing.

But, wouldn't it be great if a local church had a vision big enough to capture people's hearts and motivate them to action, so it had an impact on the community? Wouldn't it be awesome if a church was so effective people began following Jesus, growing in their faith, and as a result, the community was being loved and served? Wouldn't it be something if you could garner the combined strength of scores of believers in a local church and create an experience so powerful and compelling that hundreds met Jesus and thousands took intentional and deliberate steps toward him every week?

I love the way John 1:14 is written in *The Message*.[2] It says Christ "became flesh and blood and moved into the neighborhood." He came to us—met us where we were. In Jesus' case, the neighborhood was a rural, agricultural society in first century Palestine. He immersed himself in that culture. He wore the clothes, used the language, and illustrated his stories with the signs and symbols of the day to communicate the Gospel of an upside down kingdom here on earth.

He didn't wear God-clothes, speak God-words, and expect the culture to connect. He didn't spend years learning big words so he could impress but not communicate. He didn't look for music that was unfamiliar to the culture and expect people to learn to like it.

Jesus spent his time with real people such as Peter, James, and John, the blue-collar workers; Martha, the over-extended homemaker; Matthew, the IRS agent; and Simon, the political activist. He watched the popular culture of his day and wove it into his teaching. Jesus identified the needs of the people around him and started there as he taught.

If Jesus physically entered twenty-first century America, I believe he would do much as he did in the first century. He would hang out with normal people in the real world, and he would reserve his strongest words for the entrenched religious leaders who love their traditions more than they love their people.[3] He would leverage the culture. He would read our books, go to our movies, watch our TV shows, look at our magazines, and surf the internet so that he could better understand our culture. I believe he would look for themes in our popular culture that would help him make a connection between the topics that had our attention and the kingdom life he was offering. He would be encouraged by the lyrics in some of today's mainstream music. He would see honest searching in the words, and he would use those lyrics to reach and penetrate hearts.

I think that, just as he did in the first century, Jesus would disciple a small team of leaders while at the same time looking for opportunities to attract and influence large crowds. And when those crowds gathered, he would draw upon what he had learned about our popular culture and would use illustrations, props, and analogies that would connect his love to our hearts.

I believe that is what Jesus did and that is what he would do, and I believe he expects no less from us.

So, today, I want to stretch your thinking.

If you have bought into the belief that church is exclusively for building up the believers, I want you to reconsider.

If you think a church service cannot help believers grow AND be attractive to non-believers, I want to convince you that it can.

If you have never experienced a church service that stays true to the Bible AND is comfortable for your non-religious friends and you don't think it is even possible, I want you to explore the possibility.

If you think it is unbiblical to bring pieces of pop culture into your church services, I want you to look at some scripture with me.

If you think there is no biblical basis for using the language of our pop culture in teaching the Bible, I want to change your mind.

It is my hope this book will make you angry or make you ecstatic. I pray it gets your blood boiling with frustration or your heart beating

Dear Joe,

Just so you know, I'm not trying to change your mind. You think what you think because of the people you've met and the experiences you've had. The only thing that will change that is new experiences.

I would like, though, to try to give you hope. If judgmental Christians or boring churches frustrate you, I want you to know that is changing. If you have been hurt by churches full of people who seem to be talking to themselves and showing no interest in you, I want you to know that not all churches are like that. If you think Christians tend to deal with issues no one cares about and are clueless about the real world, you may be right. We are trying to do better, not as a manipulative tactic to win you over to the church, but because we've messed up.

It doesn't make sense for us to continue making the same mistakes over and over. You matter too much.

-Tim

fast with hope. If you walk away feeling neutral, I haven't done my job. I want you to walk away, struggle, talk, debate, and struggle some more. The community around you is dying without Jesus, and it is your God-ordained duty to wrestle until you find the best way to reach them. Once you do, don't apologize.

TIM STEVENS
March 2008

chapter 1

"MOLLY, YOUR CHURCH SUCKS!"

It is hard to exaggerate the degree to which the modern church seems irrelevant to modern man. —D. Elton Trueblood

Perhaps no one has said it better than Bono, the lead singer for U2, in an interview during the summer of 2006: "I never had any problems with Christ. But, uh, Christians were a bit of a problem for me."[1] He found that churches dealt with life on the surface, not where normal people live. It didn't line up with what he saw in the Jesus of the Bible.

That sentiment is not just the attention-grabbing words of a rock star—it is becoming the norm in America. The church is getting in the way of the Gospel. Many who call themselves Christians are like a giant black canopy over the sun keeping the world from seeing the light.

In a study published in a book called *unChristian*, authors David Kinnaman and Gabe Lyons cite six negative images that people have of Christians. In their survey of people between sixteen and twenty-nine years of age not connected with the church, they found that Christians are known as hypocritical, too focused on getting converts, homophobic, sheltered, too political, and judgmental.[2] Further, they think that Christianity is out of tune with the real-world choices, challenges, and lifestyles they face. In fact, 75 percent of those surveyed agreed that present-day Christianity could accurately be described as old-fashioned, and seven out of ten believe the faith is out of touch with reality.[3]

This is not just true on the left and right coasts, but in the Midwest as well. A woman named Deb Atkins, who had been attending our church* for just a few months, recently shared her faith story with our community. Her journey found her sitting in the parking lot

* Granger Community Church, where I have served for fourteen years, is located in northern Indiana near South Bend.

every week for more than a year, doing paperwork, while her daughter attended the service. She eventually came inside and began to take steps in relationships with others. Of her life before, she said, "I'm one of those people who thought of myself as very spiritual. But I didn't need church."* 🖥⁾

The media seems to back up that view. *USA Today* reported the results of a survey that found "A growing number of Americans are recognizing a need to develop their inner life...

> **We are too busy answering questions no one is asking.**

But many don't know where to begin, especially if they don't consider themselves 'religious.' Even if they are religious, many haven't found everything they're seeking in weekly services." The article goes on to report that the survey, by LifeWay Research, found that 86 percent said they could have a "good relationship with God without belonging to a church."[4]

How is it possible that at the same time church attendance in America is trending downward, the spiritual interest of Americans seems to be higher than ever? And while celebrities, songwriters, and movie producers are publicly talking about their spiritual questions more now than perhaps any time in history, why are they finding the church has no helpful answers for those questions? I fear it is because we are too busy answering questions no one is asking.

Researcher George Barna[†] gives four insights into why church attendance is in decline: "People avoid church because they perceive

---

* 🖥⁾ Entering the keyword "DEB" at PopGoesTheChurch.com will allow you to see her entire story on video. I've provided these interactive links throughout the book.

† I have included several quotes throughout the book from George Barna, founder of the Barna Group. He is probably the most renowned expert studying the religious beliefs and behaviors of Americans. Although I don't always agree with his conclusions, I do find his statistics very insightful.

church life as irrelevant; they have vivid memories of bad personal experiences with churches; they feel unwelcome at churches; or they lack a sense of urgency or importance regarding church life."[5]

Many churches are like restaurants where the service is lousy, the atmosphere is uncomfortable, and the food is bad. If this doesn't describe your church, it might describe the one down the street or around the corner. The bottom line of many surveys and articles and my personal observation is that most churches in America are not getting the job done. Oh, a certain group of believers might love their church, but when it comes to accomplishing the purposes of God, most churches are not cutting it. When it comes to reaching the Bonos and the Deb Atkinses and the Joes of the world—our churches are flunking.

Just last week my friends Jack and Molly* poured out their hearts to me about their church experience. They love their church in Ohio. They have been there for more than ten years now and are involved up to their eyeballs. Jack is a deacon and helps with some of the worship arts. Molly has been on the praise team and volunteers as she is able. They love their pastor and want to support him, but sadly, they would never think of inviting a friend. Not again.

They gave it a shot once. A few months earlier, Molly had invited a friend from her workplace to church. This was a close friend, and they knew she would be honest about her experience. During the entire service, Molly was wincing. She was more keenly aware than ever that the music was very bad, the message was completely irrelevant, and it was all excessively long. When she asked her friend a few days later what she thought, the answer came back, "Molly, your church sucks." It was crass and was hard to hear, but Molly knew she was right.

---

* This is a true story, but I changed the names to protect the embarrassed.

THE PURPOSE OF THE CHURCH

This is a story too often repeated. How many Christians attend a church every week they may personally enjoy, but where they would never think of inviting an unchurched friend? Many Christians are okay with that. They have decided that the purpose of the church is solely for the followers of Christ to talk about God and enjoy each other. I recently received a comment on my blog, LeadingSmart. com, from "David" who argues exactly that. He says the Bible teaches that "true church is the assembling of believers for the purpose of worshiping the Lord, studying his Word, and fellowshiping with one another."[6]

The focus of *Pop Goes the Church* is not to argue or defend the purposes of the church. But I think David is correct, but only partially. Rick Warren got it right in *The Purpose-Driven Church* when he concluded there are five unique purposes for every church. Speaking about Acts 2:42–47, Warren says, "The first Christians fellowshipped, edified each other, worshiped, ministered, and evangelized."[7] Based on the great commandment and the great commission,* Warren concludes, every church should be about these five purposes.

In America, many local churches are great at fellowship. Some are good at Bible study and worship. However, far fewer do well at moving their members into serving others, and only a tiny percentage have figured out how to evangelize—that is, help people who are far from God find their way to him.

What is the problem with evangelism? Why are local churches not doing better at reaching people with the love of Jesus? Surveys indicate that only 1 percent of Christians have the spiritual gift of evangelism.[8] That is, only one out of every one hundred followers of Christ feels comfortable personally sharing his or her faith with

---

* If you want to study this further, check out Matthew 22:37–40 for the great commandment and Matthew 28:19–20 for the great commission.

another individual. If that's not astounding enough, the number rises only slightly to eight out of every one hundred pastors who believe they have the gift of evangelism.

I can identify with that. Sharing my faith with someone makes me nervous—and I'm a pastor! Of course, you must understand, I am an introvert. I'm the guy who chooses his path to the bathroom based on passing the fewest number of people, so as not to have to engage in conversation. So the thought of talking to someone about something as personal as my faith brings sweat to my forehead. It's just hard!

I am evidently not alone. Statistically, 99 percent of you are just like me. So what are we to do? How can a church be effective at introducing people to Jesus when 99 percent of the people are afraid of those conversations and 92 percent of the pastors share the same fear?

Joe,

what do you think about this whole topic of evangelism? Does it feel like we've painted a big bull's-eye on your back and that we won't give up until we can put a checkmark in the "saved" column? I know the term "lost" isn't quite accurate when the church tries to describe people searching for a connection with God. Lost from what? Are we ever truly found? Other terms such as seekers or unchurched or non-believer aren't quite right either.

But please know we are trying, and it comes out of a heart to want to include you in the acceptance and freedom we've found in being connected to a local church.

-Tim

Most churches just keep doing what is comfortable—what they enjoy. It is just too painful to diagnose what is not working, so the leaders continue to focus on the purposes of the church, such as fellowship, worship, and Bible study, which they find easier to accomplish. Oh, they still pray for their unchurched friends. They want them to meet Jesus, but they have no idea how that might happen. Unfortunately, over time, as their Christian community becomes more ingrown, the chasm between their "lost" friends and them grows larger and larger.

One of the individuals surveyed in *unChristian* said it this way:

> So many Christians are caught up in the Christian sub-culture and are completely closed off from the world. We go to church on Wednesdays, Sundays, and sometimes on Saturdays. We attend small group on Tuesday night and serve on the Sunday school advisory board, the financial committee, and the welcoming committee. We go to barbeques with our Christian friends and plan group outings. We are closed off from the world. Even if we wanted to reach out to non-Christians, we don't have time and we don't know how.[9]

So we do what we can do and invite our friend to a church service. But we soon find out (if we didn't know already) that our church service is in an entirely different language that has no connection whatsoever to our friend. She leaves feeling bored and awkward—as if she just attended someone else's family reunion.

Is that what Jesus had in mind when he dreamed up this thing called the church? When he came to earth to give his very life so that we might experience his love and grace, do you suppose he pictured churches where the people he died to save would feel like outsiders? I have heard Mark Beeson* say it this way so often, "It has taken the church two thousand years to make Jesus—the most compelling and attractive person who ever lived—boring!" Yet thousands of churches have made "boring" an art form, and they impose their perfecting of such on people every Sunday morning.

SPIRITUALLY SEEKING

It's not that people around us aren't pursuing their faith. There is a growing percentage of people of faith in our communities who love God the best they know how—they just see the church as completely irrelevant. It does not even cross their minds to go to a church service to figure out the next spiritual step they should take. They've been to church. They've seen so-called Christians who are no different from their other friends. They have sat through one too many songs that are written like funeral dirges and talk about raising your Ebenezer (doing what to my what?). They have listened to some pastor drone on about living a sanctified life and being washed in the blood of Jesus (are these people cannibals?). So they left, without hope, still trying to figure out the answers on their own. They do this two or three times, and soon they have been burned, and they begin to pursue their faith outside the church.

But they are still spiritual beings.[10] They still want to find hope, purpose, and meaning. So they look for ways to fill the void, and often turn to the only language they really understand at their core—where they feel deeply and experience life fully. They turn to pop culture for their answers.

They turn on the radio and hear Coldplay expose their pain, singing, "When you lose something you can't replace, when you love

---

* Mark Beeson is my dear friend and senior pastor of Granger Community Church, Granger, Indiana, GCCwired.com.

someone, but it goes to waste,"[11] and it touches them. It marks them in a deeply personal way. They view a movie such as *Little Children* (2006)* and watch the tormented lives of four individuals who are trying to make sense of their humanity and yet continue to make one bad choice after another. They identify with the struggle of the actors and it moves them to take a step—to do something differently.

> The culture is actually shaping the values and faith of most people around us.

It is not that people are turning to culture just to learn a different angle about God or faith. In truth, the culture is actually shaping the values and faith of most people around us.

The authors of *A Matrix of Meaning* say this is a natural byproduct of an ineffective church:

> We embrace pop culture because we believe it offers a refreshing, alternative route to a Jesus who for many has been domesticated, declawed, and kept under wraps. As the Christian church has often adopted the role of moral policeman, pop culture has assumed the role of spiritual revolutionary, subverting and frustrating those religious authorities who desperately cling to black-and-white answers in an increasingly gray world…[12]

BOYCOTTS AND BLACK LISTS

I think that followers of Christ began to realize some time ago, perhaps subconsciously, that more and more people were pursuing God through the culture. We entered a season of boycotts, petitions,

* This was a disturbing movie that wasn't very popular, but it is worth seeing.

and black lists. Like an animal looking for its next meal, the church was driven blindly and obsessively by two primary goals. First, protect ourselves from the culture at all costs. So rather than prepare our children to engage, discern, and make good choices, we put our hands over their eyes and our fingers in their ears. However, through the internet and news media, the culture was still able to invade our homes. Unfortunately, our kids were ill prepared to deal with it.

Our second goal was to use our combined Christian power to legislate and pressure the culture to change to reflect our values. But society has changed little, and our efforts have served to further ostracize us and give every follower of Christ the feared stereotypical tag of "extremist" or "fundamentalist."

In recent years, there have been a number of books written to discuss the merging of faith and culture. It has been encouraging to see a segment of the church wake up to the potential of leveraging the culture to reach our friends. These writings are helping us learn how to negotiate relationships with the unchurched, utilize pop culture to start spiritual conversations, and be discerning so as not to pollute our own souls in the process.

But these authors almost solely focus on our personal faith. Any mention of the local church is negative or absent. It is almost as if the authors are all saying "the local church is irrelevant. It is not even a part of the conversation. If you want to have a spiritual conversation with a friend, the church will only get in your way. It must happen outside the church. Faith can be relevant. You can be relevant. But the church is not relevant, nor can it be."

Barna has concluded after years of research that no real difference exists between those who attend church and those who do not. In his book *Revolution*, Barna says, "One of the greatest frustrations of my life has been the disconnection between what our research consistently shows about churched Christians and what the Bible calls us to be."[13] He then cites seven areas, including serving the community, where those who regularly attend church are statistically no different from those who do not.*

The conclusion many seem to be making, including Barna, is to give up on the local church. He says, "We are not called to go to church. We are called to be the church."[14] I get what he means. A church exists so people will worship God, not the church, and you can accomplish the biblical purposes of the church without the organized structure of a local church. I get that.

I understand the sentiment to give up on the church. I have seen more impotent churches than effective ones. I have seen plenty of churches that "suck," and it makes me cynical. Sometimes it drowns out hope that it could ever be different.

But I have also seen churches that get it. I have seen with my own eyes what happens when the power of the local church is energized with the creativity of the arts, utilizing the language of the popular culture. I am jazzed about the spiritual longing I see in our culture. And I love what happens when faith and culture come together in the local church, so that people who were far from God hear for the first time how much they matter to him.

MY STORY

Before I continue, I must make a confession about something that colors my perspective. I know even as I write this that I can't be objective because of what I'm about to tell you. I have some church baggage (who doesn't!) that you should know about. Here it is—*I fell in love with the church before I fell in love with Jesus.* I don't know if that is good or bad. I just know it is true.

---

* So I don't leave you hanging, here are the other six areas: true worship, spiritual conversations with non-believers, intentional spiritual growth, giving, spiritual accountability, and integrating faith into family life.

Joe,

I'm afraid this story might seem a little weird to you. It kind of ventures outside of the lines of "normal" a bit, but I'm hoping you'll give me some space to share it. It is a deeply personal story that I find important to tell in order to explain my passion for a relevant church.

As you read my story, you'll find that we share something in common. I have also been frustrated with and put off by some of my church experiences. Like you, I've also had experiences with people who claimed to follow Jesus but who didn't seem to know the first thing about being a Christian. Sometimes I've even taken my eyes off my own spiritual journey and stopped taking steps because of the hypocrisy of someone else.

I guess I've come to realize there are people that will trip you up everywhere, even in church. (I know, you are thinking "especially in church.") I've just decided to do my best to stop looking at them and keep my eyes on God.

Thanks for reading my story.

-Tim

Don't get me wrong; I was no angel growing up. In fact, one of the most painful memories of my childhood was when my best friend Greg told me his dad would not let him hang with me anymore. Why? Because I was a bad influence. His dad was right. I was on a bad path. It was a wake-up call.

During the summer of 1980 when I was a young teen, God began to work on my heart. I had just finished seventh grade, and I went to a church camp in Clear Lake, Iowa, expecting it to be a week like any other. I had been going to this camp for many years, and it was always a great time to be with friends, play tennis, and talk about girls.

But this summer was different. This summer something was going on in my heart. I didn't like me, and I didn't like what I was becoming. During one of the services, I was sitting toward the back of the chapel, and at the end of the service, my legs were shaking uncontrollably. Jesus had been a part of my life since I was six years old, but this night I knew he wanted more.

That night after the service, I sat well past midnight on an old yellow school bus with Gene Bucholtz, one of the adult leaders. He was an ex-Marine with a short haircut and a huge heart for people. He saw what God was doing in my heart and began to talk with me about giving my life to the church—not just to Jesus, but devoting my life to helping others experience life change and a purpose for living. I came home that summer with new purpose, new vision.

And so began my love affair with the church. It started as a spark, but before long, it was fanned into a raging fire. I jumped in with both feet and never looked back. I am sure my parents thought about moving next door to the church since I spent hours there every day of the week. Whether it was visiting inner city kids every Saturday morning, picking them up for church on Sunday, learning how to sign for the deaf ministry, going door-to-door on visitation night, or mowing the lawn and setting up for events, my love for the church grew more intense every day.

Now, if you think I was the little boy that every mom wished for, you would be mistaken. I went through typical adolescent phases making bad choices, mouthing off to my parents, and pushing boundaries. Thankfully, my home environment and the love of my parents kept me from making any choices that had irreparable lifetime consequences.

FRUSTRATION SETS IN

While my love for the church burned hot, my love for Jesus was just beginning. As it started, an unsettled frustration grew inside me that continues to this day. There was stuff about church that I just didn't get. I didn't understand. It did not make any sense to me.

I didn't see the church being effective at helping people far from God and that didn't make sense to me. Don't get me wrong. We had walk-the-aisle invitations every time the church was open, and I saw a lot of movement in those aisles as people went down to talk with the pastor. However, it seemed like it was a lot of "I'm rededicating my life to God." (In my teenage naivety, I wondered, "How many times can someone rededicate their life before they just need to start over?") It seemed as if everyone who came forward to join the church was doing so *by transfer* from some other church.

In my years growing up, I only remember two truly *lost* adults coming to Christ at church. One was Loren Graber, who I remember because he had three very attractive daughters, and the other was Howard Sample who rode a motorcycle (which, by the way, is how I knew he was a real heathen).

That was it. You see, for us the church was a bunker. It was a place of shelter to protect Christians from the bad world out there. You didn't bring your irreligious friends to church, if by chance you had any. No, you got them saved *out there*—and when they had been cleaned up, you brought them to the place of refuge.

We even had one of those printed signs above every exit door. It said, "You Are Now Entering the Mission Field." I guess it was a good sign. It reminded us that it is not just about us—we need to think about others—but why out there? Why couldn't I bring a *lost* friend to church? Why did he have to be won outside the doors of the church, and only brought to church after he had been cleaned up and was ready to grow? I didn't understand.

When I was about fourteen years old, we had a visitor at church on Sunday morning. He was not with someone else; he was by himself. Very unusual, but stranger yet, he was very unclean, had ratty tennis shoes on, and I remember seeing his dirty toes showing through the holes in his shoes. As a young teen trying to learn, I stood close by and listened to the ushers discuss what they were going to say to him. I overheard one usher say, "This is God's house, and he can't dress that way. We at least need to find him a different pair of shoes before the service starts." I don't know what they eventually said to him, but I never saw him again. I didn't get that.

Of course, it's not as if bringing an unchurched person to church would have worked anyway. The services at my church were perfectly designed for someone who had always gone to church and always known Jesus. It was the perfect Petri dish environment for people like me who grew up in the church and needed to grow in our faith, but it did not work for *normal* people.

Another time, my youth pastor gave me the opportunity to preach on a Sunday evening. It went okay, but when I was finished, I was told by one of the pastors never to teach out of any Bible except the King James Version again. Huh? I had mistakenly thought the goal was communication, that we wanted people to *understand*. Little did I know the priority was speaking the King's English. It did not make sense.

When I was fifteen, I was asked to put together a slide show about our inner city ministries. I chose a song called "People Need the Lord" by Steve Green—a song that had a great message and grabbed your emotions but had no drums. I figured it was safe. After programming the show, I was told his voice was too raspy and too sensual, and I was given a scratchy-sounding cassette tape of an off-pitch women's trio to use instead. The goal obviously was not effectiveness.

Over and over through these experiences and many more, I was learning that church was totally irrelevant to the world. As foreign as a Korean-speaking service would be to most Americans, my church (and every other church I was aware of) was culturally missing the boat in impacting the

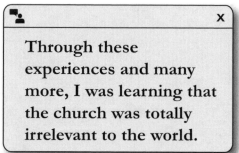

Through these experiences and many more, I was learning that the church was totally irrelevant to the world.

community around it. They weren't speaking the language and did not even know it.

But I am so glad I grew up in that church. Not only did I get some real grounding in scripture (for which I am thankful), but this frustration with relevance in the church turned into a passion, an obsession really, to build a church that could make a difference in a community.

IS CHANGE POSSIBLE?

During my years serving in that church (and others since), my love for Jesus began to grow. I moved from doing stuff *for* the church to experiencing the one for whom I was doing it. The more I served Jesus, the more I grew in my relationship with him.

I began to wonder—is it possible to have a church that isn't boring? What would happen if you could find a church where the Bible comes alive? What would happen if your church service used words that normal people could understand? What would happen if the music were familiar and made sense? What would happen if you addressed issues that people really care about, that could really make their lives different? What would happen if you had a church where you could invite a friend and there would be a good chance that he or she could understand and begin to experience an inner life change?

Since those years in the early '80s, there has been a lot of talk about *relevant* church services. Bill Hybels* has led the way in a conversation about being *seeker-sensitive*, and thousands of churches have begun to consider what it would be like to offer a church service that is relevant, easy to understand, and not offensive to a seeker. That has been a great thing. This conversation has taken place in probably every church in this country and many around the world, and thousands of congregations have made changes. Some have made small, hardly perceptible shifts, while others have radically changed the focus of their ministries. Even churches that have chosen to hang on to their traditions have been helped by the conversation about the unchurched around them.

But I'm not just talking about being seeker-sensitive. It is not only about being relevant. It is not about having a contemporary service with drums and guitars or adding drama to your line-up.

I want to take the conversation a step further. It is about turning around, staring your culture straight in the face, and leveraging that culture to reach people for Christ. It is about bringing pieces of the culture into the church in order to make the Bible understood, and highlighting where biblical principles are already present in pop culture. It is about *not* giving up on the church but changing our view of church from the inside out so that we begin to see life-transformational changes in our communities.

It is about getting out of our holy huddles, turning around and looking real people right in the eyes, seeing the lives they live and the problems they encounter (as messy and unholy as they might be). It is about celebrating parts of pop culture where there are signs of spiritual interest. It is about building churches that focus more on preparing

---

* Bill Hybels is the lead pastor of Willow Creek Community Church in South Barrington, Illinois, and author of several books including *Rediscovering Church*. I am a better leader because of his influence on me.

followers to live in the culture and leverage the culture rather than criticizing and building walls of protection around our commune-like congregations.

Since that night on the yellow school bus in 1980 when I knew Jesus wanted more, I have had a growing passion to see people change through the local church. It isn't because my love for the church* overshadows my love for Jesus. No, on the contrary, it is because of my love for Jesus that I still have hope for the church. My goal is to reignite that love affair in your life as well—to see you find new hope in the power of the local church. To open your mind to new thoughts about the language that is required in order to reach real people in a real world. If we keep doing what we have always done, we will keep getting what we have always gotten—and I am not satisfied with that.

To get started, we have to watch our language...

---

* Just to be clear, there is nothing wrong with being in love with the church. We learn in Ephesians 5:25 that Jesus loved the church and gave himself up for her.

chapter 2

LOST IN TRANSLATION

According to BrandChannel.com, a few years ago Pepsi attempted to translate its motto, "Come Alive: You're in the Pepsi Generation," into Chinese. The result came across as something like "Pepsi brings your ancestors back from the dead." That is a strong promise—or threat, depending on which ancestors we are talking about.

Pepsi has not been the only company with language problems. Microsoft's operating system, Vista, turned out to be a disparaging term for a frumpy old woman in Latvia. (All this time I've been yelling out, "Hey, frumpy old woman in Latvia!" I could have been saying, "Hey, Vista.") In addition, Motorola's Hello Moto ringtone sounds like "Hello, Fatty" in India.[1]

It all comes down to a language problem. It doesn't matter how good your intentions are; if what you are saying is lost in translation, then your message isn't going to get through. Sounds basic, doesn't it? Yet we see this principle violated every day.

When is the last time you were talking to a technician about (you fill in the blank), and he was less than helpful:

> The problem, Mrs. Walshowitz, is in the combo-flixty valve. It's probably because you turned this knob and hit this button at the same time, right? (Now he turns to you with a half-smile and superior look.) Well, as you know, when you do that, the kinetic energy is transferred from the gated techno-flube into the ventrifugal reflective shadometer, which forces a nettlebonic charge through the system and (chuckle), and we all know what happens then...

As you look at this clueless geek,* you realize he has no idea he

---

* Notice to all geeks...this is not a slam. I am one of you! Anything that plugs in, has knobs and levers, and some flashing LED lights gets my attention. This particular geek was clueless... but that doesn't mean you are!

is speaking another language. Unfortunately, this scenario is repeated over and over in so-called *customer service* interactions every day of our lives.

Sometimes, we are the ones at fault. Several years ago, I was in Albania with Mark Beeson as we were exploring a mission's partnership. Mark had a last-minute opportunity to speak in an auditorium full of students at the University of Tirana. This was just a few years after communism had fallen, and citizens were still not allowed to leave Albania freely. (In fact, people wanted so desperately to leave that the government instituted a lottery where instead of receiving money, the winners received a passport to leave the country.) However, on this day, Mark was speaking to university students who were born in Albania and who had never left the country.

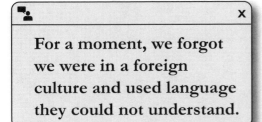

> For a moment, we forgot we were in a foreign culture and used language they could not understand.

He preached a tremendous message and the students loved him. But there was a point in his message, spoken through an interpreter, when he gave an illustration that didn't connect. "How many of you have been ice skating?" he asked the audience. Not a hand rose in the room. Even the interpreter was confused. You see, they lived in a climate that rarely got below freezing, and thus had never seen ice skating. Many had never even heard of ice skating. For a moment, we forgot we were in a foreign culture and used language they could not understand.

Another time I was with Mark Waltz* in a remote village in central India. It was Sunday morning and we were attending church, but this

---

* Mark Waltz is a pastor at Granger Community Church, author of *First Impressions: Creating Wow Experiences at Your Church*, and a good friend.

wasn't any *normal* church you might picture. This church was one very small room with no windows or doors and a dirt floor. The men were seated on the ground on the right side, and the women were on the ground on the left side, where several of them were openly breast-feeding their babies.

As we entered, we were ushered to the front of the room and seated in some dilapidated pastors' throne chairs facing the audience of thirty or forty people. We were introduced and asked quite unexpectedly to preach a message. They turned to me first. I did what any good friend would do and stood up, greeted the people, and introduced Mark Waltz (to his surprise) who would be delivering that day's message.

With no time to prepare, he taught (through an interpreter) from a passage he had read earlier that morning. He talked about Ephesians 1 and said the Holy Spirit has been given to us as a guarantee. To try to communicate better, he used this illustration, "It's kind of like when you go to the bank and deposit your money so that you can get a good interest rate."

I watched their faces. They weren't tracking. Bank? Money? Interest? It made no sense and had no connection to their very simple, third-world lives. Even the babies stopped eating for a moment and cocked their heads at Mark in bewilderment.

I wish I could say this only happens to my friends, but that would not be true. I also have had my share of *lost in translation* moments. One of the first I remember as an adult was when I was the manager of a traveling road team for Life Action Ministries. The team included adults, ranging in age from eighteen years to thirty-something. At twenty years old, I was definitely one of the younger ones, but I had been given some big leadership responsibilities. I know there were some older people on the team just waiting for me to mess up.

I did not disappoint them. We were in Texas, and getting ready to head to Houston for a series of meetings. I had gone ahead to visit with the pastor to talk through some last minute details. He had been hospitalized for a couple of days, so our meeting took place in his hospital room.

For some background, you should know that I was young, naïve, and sheltered and had never heard of prostate cancer. Yes, I'm serious. I didn't even have any idea where the prostate was located. This pastor was having surgery done on his prostate and was also having some work done on the tendons in his wrist. Unrelated procedures, obviously, but I didn't know that at the time.

When I came back the next day, I met with the team to brief them on our daily schedule and tell them about my visit with this pastor.

I let them know the pastor was in the hospital, but "he is still in a little pain from the prostate work they did on his wrist."

That was it. I lost total control of the meeting. People were rolling around on the floor laughing their heads off—and I stood there in the front of the room, exposed for what I was—a kid who was getting his feet wet in leadership. Later, when I was given an anatomy lesson, I laughed at myself too. But I also learned a valuable lesson about language that day. In this case, my mistake wasn't using language the people did not understand. I was trying to connect to my crowd but was using language that *I* did not understand.

These stories and many others have been relived hundreds of times and given my friends and me moments of unrestrained laughter, but it is exactly what many of our American church services sound like to someone who did not grow up going to church. We use words, illustrations, and analogies that are very commonplace to us, but for the *outsider*, it is like talking about interest rates to someone who has never heard of a bank.

THE CURSE OF KNOWLEDGE

The problem is not our heart. It is not our intentions. We are ignorant. We don't mean to be ignorant, but we are. We have a disease called "The Curse of Knowledge."

In their book *Made to Stick*, brothers Chip Heath and Dan Heath expand on this term, "Once we know something, we find it hard to imagine what it was like not to know it. Our knowledge has 'cursed' us. And it becomes difficult for us to share our knowledge with others, because we can't readily re-create our listeners' state of mind."[2]

We are cursed with church knowledge. We know the basics of the Bible. We know where to park our car in order to exit quickly. We know where the bathrooms are located. We know the songs. We know when we are supposed to clap after a song and when we should be reflective. We know what the pastor means when he says, "Just as in the days of Noah..." We know we ALWAYS sing verse, chorus, verse, chorus, bridge, chorus, repeat last phrase, again, one more time. We know God is faithful AND all things work out for good AND sometimes God answers prayer by telling us to wait AND when God closes a door he sometimes opens a window AND a thousand other silly slogans that look good on a bumper sticker but mean nothing to people who do not know.

The problem is we have no memory of what it is not to know. And so our churches, led by people plagued with the curse of knowledge, provide experiences and design services that feel right to people who know stuff but totally miss the boat when it comes to people who don't.

We have to speak the language. This isn't a new concept, is it? In fact, I am guessing some of you right now are mentally saying, "Yada, yada, yada. I have been hearing this for years. Tell me something new."

When we hear "speak the right language," many of us think about

Joe,

I'm just curious. Do those little cutesy Christian bumper stickers bug you as much as they do me? When you see, "Got Jesus? It's Hell without Him," do you want to hurl as I do? What do you think when you walk past one car that says, "God Is my Co-Pilot" and the next one that reads, "If God Is Your Co-Pilot... switch seats"?

Here's the truth: when I see a bumper sticker that says something such as "Too Blessed To Be Depressed" or "This Car Is Prayer-Conditioned," I'm embarrassed. I'm afraid someone like you is going to see it and write off all Christians as clueless. The people who buy those stickers are well meaning. They just have the curse of knowledge and don't even know it.

Maybe I can convince them to put the stickers on their refrigerators rather than on their cars. I'll work on that.

-Tim

the church revolution of the 1990s called the "seeker movement." Although there were many variations, this movement said, "Be aware there are people in the room who are not yet convinced—they are seeking." So we began to change some of the words, added a drama, and introduced contemporary music to our line-up.

This has been helpful, but it's more than those few changes. The truth is, a church can have well-acted drama, amazing video, excellent contemporary music, and language that is sensitive—and still just be communicating an irrelevant message that the unchurched cannot possibly understand.

The curse of knowledge disables most of us (who have been in church for years) from being able to hear our message in the same way as someone who has no room for church in their lives. It also keeps us from hearing the teaching of Jesus in the same way someone who did not grow up in the church hears the same words.

The curse of knowledge keeps us from being able to see that we are not communicating. You say, "I'm speaking in English. Everyone in my community understands English. I'm speaking in their language. Right?" Not necessarily. Speaking the right language is more than the words that are spoken. It is about context, timing, previous experiences, and culture.

Speaking the right language is about understanding filters.

THE INVISIBLE GLASSES WE ALL WEAR

In the 2004 movie *National Treasure,* Ben (played by Nicolas Cage) is on a search for buried treasure. Along the way, he discovers a pair of ocular glasses invented by Benjamin Franklin. These glasses have several different colored filters that can be rotated down in front of the lens and which are supposed to help him decode the map that has been hidden on the back of the Declaration of Independence (a very believable story, don't you think?).

Ben uses the glasses to help him find a building, which he later decides must be a dead-end. He is about to give up when he realizes that if he uses a different combination of the filters, he sees entirely different hidden markings on the map and is ultimately able to find the hidden treasure.

Benjamin Franklin did not invent our filters, but they are important nonetheless. Filters are those invisible shaded glasses we all wear that give us a view of the world different from anyone else. Everyone wears them, but no two pairs are alike. Your filters are different from mine; mine are different from yours. Even if you have a twin

ANOTHER PERSPECTIVE ON FILTERS

We have to understand that language, by its very nature, is subjective. When you hear the phrase 'old barn,' for example, what image comes to mind? Instantly, and without any prompting from me, you began searching your memory banks for a photo of an old barn. The exact picture that you accessed in your memory archives depends on your past and current life experience.

So, what does the phrase 'old barn' bring to your mind? Is it a memory from childhood, when you and a friend explored an abandoned old barn that became a secret clubhouse or a place for hiding treasures? Maybe you grew up on a farm and have firsthand knowledge of old barns, or perhaps you pictured a photo spread in *Architectural Digest* showing a spectacular home created from a renovated old barn. Maybe the first image that came to mind was from last night's rerun of *Little House on the Prairie* that your seven-year-old daughter was watching or the DVD rental of *Cold Mountain* you watched this past weekend. The point is that whatever image came to mind, your understanding of the phrase 'old barn' is based entirely on your life experience. If you had never seen an old barn, your memory banks would be empty, and the phrase would have no meaning to you. The words we use have no raw definitions. Instead, from our life experiences, we fill up mental containers—containers of understanding and meaning—that we call words. In addition, because your life experience is different from my life experience, the connotations of words—our understanding of what those words mean—will vary from person to person.[3]

—Ron Martoia in *Static*

who has never left your side, you wear different filters. Oh, some of your filters might be the same, but the totality of all your filters is as unique to you as your DNA. We see the world differently from anyone else because he or she hasn't shared the same life story. We see life uniquely because of our upbringing, education, ethnicity, hurts, and experiences.

We are wearing our filters all the time—when we hear information, meet someone new, or have a conversation with an individual. Everything is viewed or heard through our filters. Yet most of the time, we are not aware of our own, and rarely do we think about other people's filters. Yet every person we ever meet has many of them in place.

Think about it. Someone who was raised in an abusive environment does not understand you when you talk about loving parents. They think you are clueless. They have a **family filter** that is different from yours. Someone who was abandoned by a parent might strongly believe that you are damaging your children if you spank them. Their **parenting filter** dictates their behavior and their judgment of those who don't agree.

Some people have very strong feelings that are rooted in their experience about consumer products. For example, the mention of Apple computers will cause some readers to experience an increased heart rate and desire to run to the nearest Apple Store to lay down a lot of money for their next purchase. Others find it all quite curious and can't imagine why people pay so much money for bells and whistles. (The first group is now enraged that I reduced the appeal of Apple computers to bells and whistles. I know I'm going to get some e-mails!) For some, the mention of an airline where you recently had a bad experience suddenly yanks you back to that traumatic day. You have a **consumer filter** that colors your ability to listen to the rest of the conversation.

We all have some type of **relational filter** in place. Some individuals have experienced much rejection, and so in every interaction, they assume they will be rejected again. This filter affects their emotional response and prevents them from having close relationships. They end up pushing away the very thing they long for the most. Others have never experienced unconditional love and so come across very leech-like in their relationships.

A LESSON ON FILTERS FROM COLUMBINE

One British reporter recognized the power of filters as various groups assigned blame for the shootings at Columbine High School in 1999:

> The religious right blamed what happened on the federal ban on prayer in the schools. The internet, where one of the suspects had a web site, was severely criticized, as were violent movies, television shows, and video games. Child psychologists were happy to talk about how we don't encourage boys to share their feelings...The anti-gun lobby used the shootings to rail against the easy access to guns. But the pro-gun lobby, incredibly, blamed the shooting deaths of the 15 people on the fact that we don't have enough guns...[4]

It was evident that the filters over the eyes of the person casting the blame determined who was blamed.

Most American adults have some kind of **church filter**. Some think all pastors are dishonest. Others think all pastors abuse children. Many people have the filter that says every church is just out for money. Maybe it is the first time in two years the pastor has ever mentioned the offering, but their response is, "See! The church is all about money!" They respond through their filter.

I don't know what invisible filters you wear. I just know you have some. All of us wear multiple filters. Everyone attending your church has filters in place. That is why you can attend church with two friends who have very different reactions to the same service. One woman will say it changed her life, while the guy next to her says it was the worst message he has ever heard. You wonder, "Did they even attend the same church?" Yes, they did. They are just looking through different filters.

I haven't mentioned one filter yet. In fact, it is rarely talked about and yet I bet it affects 99.9 percent of everyone you will ever meet. This filter is huge in today's society—in fact, so many people look through this filter that it has an impact on our entire culture. This filter not only influences those who don't go to church—it also has a significant impact, more than we would like to admit, on those who attend church every week.

In most families, this filter will have a greater impact on a child's choices and values than the parents will. This filter will influence how a teen thinks about authority and morality more than his or her youth pastor will be able to. It is through this filter that relational choices are made, right and wrong is determined, faith is explored, questions are raised, authority is challenged, and mistrust is encouraged.

The filter is *pop culture*. (I know, you already guessed, but you cheated by looking at the title of this book.) And unpacking the extraordinary impact of pop culture on our communities and our churches will take an entire chapter. So turn the page.

chapter 3

WHY POP CULTURE
IS SO POPULAR

The world of entertainment and mass communications—through television, radio, contemporary music, movies, magazines, art, video games and pop literature—is indisputably the most extensive and influential theological training system in the world.

—George Barna

The term *popular culture* is relatively new and was initially a reactionary term to high culture. *High culture* referred to works that were of the highest sophistication and quality. An orchestra playing Tchaikovsky would qualify as high culture, whereas a different group of instruments playing something that sounded like Metallica would not make the cut. High culture was experienced by and for those who were elitists, typically in the upper class.

What about the rest of us? The term popular culture started as a definition of the entertainment options of the average person—everything that wasn't considered *high* culture. However, in the past fifty years, the definition has changed, and now it is known to refer to anything in culture that is popular. Scholars explain, "Popular culture requires a mass audience created by urbanization and democratization along with technologies of mass distribution; in other words, mass media in all forms."[1]

What the heck does that mean? Here is a definition of popular culture in my simple, non-intellectual terms: *Pop culture is the world of music, movies, television shows, books, magazines, fashion, sports, art, video games, and the internet that has a following and acceptance by millions around the globe.*

Back in the early 1900s, it was not called "popular culture," simply because it wasn't popular. It really had very limited impact. You didn't even experience it unless you lived near a big city and had the money to see a symphony or experience an opera. Then in 1903, they began making moving picture films in Hollywood and the world began to change—slowly at first. It wasn't until 1927 that the first movie was presented with synchronized sound and that was years before there were enough theaters around to be accessible to small-town America. Still, culture was *out there*. You had to go somewhere to access it. It had not yet entered our homes—not until the age of television.

Beginning in the 1940s with black and white, and then in 1954 with the first NBC nationwide broadcast in color, the popular culture began to get closer and closer. At around the same time, cable television was growing in subscribers as an alternative to small communities that weren't close enough to the limited number of broadcast signals.

In 1972, everything began to change much more rapidly. That is when Charles Dolan and Gerald Levin launched the first pay-TV network called Home Box Office (HBO).[2] This was followed soon by the Turner Broadcasting System (WTBS), and by the end of the 1970s, more than sixteen million households were paying for pop culture to enter their living rooms. By 1989, the number had increased to fifty-three million households that subscribed to cable television and seventy-seven additional networks had joined HBO and WTBS.

Pop culture was solidly in our homes, and it wasn't going away. In the early 1990s, we saw the internet begin to take off and a short time later, cell phones[*] became widely used. Pop culture had taken another step—not just into our homes, but also into our bedrooms, our cars, our jobs, our schools, our—well, our everywhere.

Today, the average American home has more television sets than it has people. Half of the homes in America have more than three television sets, and in the average home, the television is on eight hours and fourteen minutes each day.[3] A typical person watches television twenty-eight hours a week—by the time he or she is sixty-five

---

* Anyone who has a teenager knows that pop culture has entered the world of cell phones through ringtones, multimedia, and MP3 capabilities.

years old, he or she will have spent nine years watching his or her favorite shows.[4]

Additionally, the average person spends thirty-one hours and twenty-five minutes each month surfing the internet.[5] Americans downloaded or purchased 1.5 billion songs in 2006.[6] And at the box office, we spent $9.4 billion on movie tickets to see more than six hundred films that were released in 2006.[7] In all of these media, we are inundated with advertising. The *New York Times Magazine* reported in early 2007 "the average city dweller is exposed to 5,000 ads per day."[8]

IT IS A NEW DAY

Recognizing the pervasiveness and influence of pop culture requires us to accept that we live in a new day. It is not the industrial age. It is not the modern generation. We live squarely in the middle of a media-driven, entertainment-crazed world. People around us are not only watching and listening—they are actually shaping their values through the movies, books, songs, and TV shows that fill their world. We can get angry about that. We can throw a tantrum, sign a petition, and support a boycott. That's all fine and dandy. But it won't change the facts. The influence of pop culture is here, and it is here to stay.

And it is having a drastic impact on the way the people around us pursue and experience their faith. Prior to around forty years ago, there was no question about where you would go for answers about religion. You would go to your pastor. You would find a church to attend. If you were beginning to feel a stir in your heart that there must be something more in this life (i.e., you were having a religious experience), you trotted off to the closest church and found your answers—but not anymore.

Toward the end of the last century, two things happened in our culture that significantly reduced the power and influence of the

WHY POP CULTURE IS SO POPULAR

organized church. The first I have already explained—the introduction of popular culture into our homes and corresponding access of information through the internet.

The second was several very public scandals involving several religious leaders, beginning in 1986 with Jim and Tammy Faye Bakker, followed in 1987 with Oral Roberts, and in 1988 with Jimmy Swaggart. It

Joe,

I imagine when you see a famous Christian leader, who is known for having strong family values, fall in the very area they preached against, you might want to categorize all Christians as fakes. I'm guessing it may even cause you to mistrust every church leader immediately.

I don't blame you. In fact, the Bible in matthew 7:15 warns us about leaders who are fakes. They are called "wolves in sheep's clothing." I like that analogy.

I just encourage you not to put every leader in the same corner as those who have failed publicly. Thousands of pastors live with high integrity. That may be hard for you to imagine, but I've met a bunch of them and worked with a few. They aren't without fault, but they live authentic lives and build safeguards around themselves to keep from going down a bad path.

I know it's difficult to trust again once you've been burned. Lately, whenever a Christian leader falls, I try to remember to whisper a prayer for those who are still standing.

-Tim

didn't stop there. Soon the Catholic Church was in the spotlight with scandalous accusations of sexual abuse by priests against small children. If you think these types of scandals are yesterday's news, just review the headlines from 2006 to see the embarrassing fall of Ted Haggard, well-known pastor in Colorado and leader of the National Association of Evangelicals.

The first five words in the book *unChristian* sum it up quite succinctly, "Christianity has an image problem."[9] The respect in the community that was prevalent for *men of the cloth* for decades is nothing but a memory. It may be present in reruns of *Little House on the Prairie,* but it has no foundation in our current reality.

At the same time, people haven't stopped pursuing the God-shaped void in their lives. They haven't stopped asking questions or groping for answers. Most of them just don't go to pastors, priests, and churches for help anymore. Instead, they go to the First Church of the Open Cinema to watch and hear the latest message by Steven Spielberg or Oliver Stone. Rather than call their pastor, they flip on afternoon television and catch America's favorite spiritualist, Oprah Winfrey, or they develop their theology based on the lyrics of artists such as U2, Coldplay, and Carrie Underwood.

> **Church people often wrongly assume that those who don't go to church are not spiritual.**

George Barna says, "A growing number of Americans are shifting away from conventional church experiences and gravitating toward alternative expressions of faith."[10]

"If you study the statistics, the typical modern American is much more likely to be exposed to a new religious insight or doctrine at the mall or the movie multiplex than in a traditional sanctuary," says nationally syndicated columnist Terry Mattingly. "This is how modern Americans spend their time, spend their money, and make their decisions. Day by day, they have evolved into mass-media disciples."[11]

Church people often wrongly assume that those who don't go to church are not spiritual. How could they be? We can't imagine how that is even possible. We have a filter that says, "People who are spiritual go to church, and people who don't go to church are not spiritual." It is very difficult for us to consider that there are people in our communities who *never* go to church—not even at Christmas and Easter—yet are deeply spiritual people.

Mattingly says, "I think that few truly recognize that moviegoers are wrestling with religious issues week after week when, to paraphrase the great American film director Frank Capra, they sit listening to sermons in dark theaters."[12] Richard Leonard, a Jesuit priest from Australia, said, "The multiplex is the modern market for ideas and values. It is shaping us, whether we like it or not."[13]

The influence will only increase as those who have grown up under the inescapable shadow of pop culture continue to age. David Kinnaman reports:

> Americans of all ages are inundated with media and entertainment options. Yet [16- to 29-year-olds] consume more hours of media from more sources than do older generations. Many immensely enjoy the latest hot movie, music, website, or pop culture buzz. Technologies connect young people to information and each other—and power their self-expression and creativity—in ways older adults do not fully appreciate.[14]

I am not suggesting that a search for spirituality is equal to taking steps toward Christ. I don't assume that just because movie producers or songwriters explore spiritual issues in their art that they are pursuing a relationship with Jesus. They might be far from that. I am merely saying that at the same time Christianity has lost its influence, pop culture has taken its place. To ignore this fact means losing a tremendous potential to help people connect the dots back to a relationship with Jesus.

And this is not just an issue facing those outside the church. Even those who attend church every week struggle to understand the power of culture. They can sit through a boring sermon and feel nothing, while being moved deeply after watching a television show or going to a movie. Or they realize that after a year of church services, they cannot point to one thing in their lives that is different. Yet a song or television interview or a sixty-second commercial can speak to them so strongly they immediately change their lifestyle to help someone in need. Where is the fruit of a life connected to Jesus seen more so than when we help someone less fortunate?

Pastors have not done a good job of helping their congregations navigate the whirling waters of culture. Detweiler and Taylor add:

> Frustration, confusion, and guilt can cripple those
> desperately trying to harmonize the Bible with their
> everyday lives. They want to understand how the
> same God can speak to them through R-rated films
> such as *The Shawshank Redemption* or *Braveheart* while
> calling them to "flee from sexual immorality."
> (1 Cor 6:18)[15]

Somehow, our theology has taught us that God speaks only at church. He only talks to us through his written word or through an individual (aka pastor or priest) who has been trained. That belief is very confusing to us when we feel God tugging at our heart through the culture.

Yes, we've been taught about the power of the Holy Spirit and about how he can prompt you 24/7. But in reality, many of us were never given any context for God speaking to us through a secular song, a blockbuster movie, or a graphic novel. Is it possible? What do we do with it? How do we respond?

MY FIRST MOVIE AT AGE 26

I grew up in an environment where going to the movie theater was wrong and listening to music with a driving beat was a sin. I very vividly remember going to the concert (without permission, of course) of a Christian rock singer when I was eighteen years old. I was shocked to find out God was there! I felt his presence as much that night as any time previously in my life. Yet this was supposed to be sin. How is that possible? It made no sense to me as a teen trying to figure out what I believed. There wasn't a *God-speaking-to-me-through-music-with-a-beat* category in my brain.

I guess my experience is not that rare. Hollywood actor Brad Pitt confessed recently, "I'd go to Christian revivals and be moved by the Holy Spirit, and I'd go to rock concerts and feel the same fervor. Then I'd be told, 'That's the devil's music! Don't partake in that!'"[16]

I remember my first experience in a movie theater. It was 1994 and I was twenty-six years old (yes, I am serious). I don't remember much about the movie but I remember this overwhelming feeling that this was what I was made for—no, not watching that particular movie, which, by the way, was *Star Trek: Generations*. But that night my mind was opened to exploring the power of this incredible medium that combined the senses of sound, sight, smell, taste, and touch. I was experiencing the power of movie magic, best described by

William Romanowski when he asks:

> How is it that when we enter into the world of a film
> we can become emotionally engaged, even moved
> profoundly, while fully aware at the same time that
> what is being presented to us never actually hap-
> pened and is not happening now, that the characters
> and events we're seeing exist only as a product of
> imagination?[17]

What an overwhelming experience to have for the first time as an adult! I don't think God was speaking to me through Jean-Luc Picard or Data, but I did have a sense there was power in this medium—that this tool could be used for good. However, I didn't have a category for that either. My theology didn't allow it.

It took years of deconstructing what I thought I knew, asking questions, reading books, studying the Bible, praying, thinking, and searching to bring me down the path that has led to the thoughts in this book. If you look at it on the surface of my background, I am probably the most unlikely person to be writing a book about leverag-ing pop culture in the local church. Yet I think the exposure to *doing church* while being oblivious to the culture gave me such a passion to see it change.

BREAKING IT DOWN

I am a get-to-the-bottom-line type of guy, so let's break it down. What have we determined so far?

People in our culture are searching for God.

The church has failed them in this search due to A) the inability of churches to speak a language people can understand, and B) the public failures of a few high profile church leaders, which has cast doubt on all.

So people are searching for answers in pop culture whether they realize it or not, which eventually shapes their faith and values.

What happens next is crucial. Every church has a choice about what to do with this information. And every church *is* making a choice, whether intentionally or not. Whether they have thought through the consequences or they are blindly doing what they have always done, every group of Christ-followers is deciding what they will do with the realities that surround them.

Not too long ago, in a small Midwestern town, five churches had to make this very choice...

chapter 4

A TALE OF FIVE CHURCHES

Everyone was talking about it. I don't just mean most people; I mean everyone in this small town in eastern Nebraska was buzzing about the big news of the summer. Truth be told, it was the biggest thing to happen in these parts in years. It seemed like the only news Glenmoor, Nebraska, ever received was of one more plant closing the doors and leaving town. There were only twenty thousand people left in a town that had twice that many residents just ten years ago. But now, there was some excitement in the air. There was a sense of anticipation that lined every conversation.*

About three months ago, the rumors had started to fly. At first, it was hardly believable, and most people dismissed it after a few moments of giddy "what if" conversation. The idea of those people coming here, to their town, seemed implausible. It was fun to dream about, but it surely wouldn't happen.

But then, last week, the mayor confirmed it during his speech before the Memorial Day parade. Following a drum roll from the local high school marching band, he made the huge announcement and the entire town cheered loud enough that they were sure to be heard in the next county over. It was confirmed; it was no rumor!

And it was even better than expected. Not only would Tom Cruise be here, in their town, staying in their hotels, eating in their restaurants—he would be staying for three months! It had just been announced by Paramount that they were making a movie on location in none other than Glenmoor, Nebraska. And not just any movie—this would be a big-budget blockbuster, starring not only Tom Cruise, but also Rene Russo, Tom Wilkinson, Ali Larter, and others.

"Why make a movie in Glenmoor?" some asked.

A few quickly replied, "Who cares? Just be grateful and quit asking questions!" Others took more time to answer and said the director wanted to make the movie entirely in Glenmoor to make sure it had that Midwest, small-town feeling. The movie needed to be believable.

Regardless of the reason, the thought of what this would mean for the town was astounding. For three months, they would have national attention. There

---

* This is an allegory, and as such, any similarity to real towns, churches, or pastors is entirely coincidental (although quite possibly divine).

would be hundreds of crew and cast members (the mayor said more than six hun-
dred) living in their community. This might be the very thing they needed to kick-
start the economy and get the momentum moving in a positive direction again.

In the coming weeks, more details about the film plot began to emerge. It would
be an R-rated movie about a factory worker who loses his job and begins a string
of illicit affairs that lead him on a path of self-discovery. Not exactly a family
film, but it would take more than that to squelch the excitement in the town.

It wasn't long, however, until some of the churches in town began to weigh in
with their response to this news. A few responded quite predictably, while others
surprised everyone.

Pop culture has permeated every community in America, and most around the globe, regardless of how big or small, urban or rural, crowded or remote. Your town might not have Tom Cruise coming to make a movie, but it has the influence of Angelina Jolie, Rihanna, Justin Timberlake, Tom Clancy, Will Smith, Howard Stern and ten thousand others like them every day over the airwaves, on the big screen, through a cable, across the web, on billboards, and even directly to your teen's ringtone.

> **Every church makes a choice in how to respond to the pop culture, and the choice it makes determines how much of an impact it will have on its community.**

The question is not, "Does pop culture have an influence?" The question is, "What am I going to do with it? How will I respond? What choice will I make?"

Every church makes a choice in how to respond to the pop culture, and the choice it makes determines how much of an impact it will have on its community.

CONDEMN THE CULTURE

One of the first to come out with passion and energy against the film was Pastor Bill Jackson from Grace Church. He was outraged at the city officials for their sponsorship of the project. He was disappointed with the city folk for blindly accepting it. And he was angry at the movie industry for continuing to produce smut such as this that was tearing at the very fabric of the society. "It is bad enough that you are making it in Hollywood—but keep it out of my hometown!" he yelled.

He began to rally his congregation to voice their concerns. Every time he had an opportunity and a crowd he asked, "Why do we want to bring this filth from Hollywood into our community—one that is known for its family values?" When that idea didn't seem to be getting traction, he encouraged his congregation to vote with their checkbook. He was able to obtain a list of every vendor in town who was providing hotel rooms, meals, or other services for the film crew, and he published this list for his congregation.

"You can do what you want, but my family won't be giving any of our money to these businesses who are mindlessly aligning themselves with that which is evil!" he preached on the Sunday the list was distributed.

As a teen, I remember attending the ordination of a young pastor in central Iowa. He sat on the stage all alone while a group of about twenty older (and presumably wiser) pastors peppered him with theological questions, one after another. The day is pretty much a blur in my memory, but I recall one question that was asked by a pastor who was probably nearing eighty years old.

"Which attribute of God is stronger—his holiness or his love?"

I am guessing I remember that question so well because of the ensuing conversation I overheard during the lunch break. It was then another pastor asked, "Bob, why do you ask that question at every single ordination? And, if you are so curious about the question, how come you never push back on the answer?"

"I don't have any idea what the correct answer is," Bob replied. "I just want to make sure every young pastor is struggling with the question."

If this elder pastor who had been studying the Bible for more than sixty years didn't know the answer, I'm not going to pretend to have a handle on it. But it seems to me that this desire to condemn the culture comes out of an imbalance toward the holiness side.

Joe,

If you saw any news reports about the highly publicized boycotts of Disney or 7-Eleven, or the recent one against Ford motor Company, you may believe every church and every Christian in the world is in support of these causes. That surely is how it comes across in the media. I'm not saying the sponsors of the boycotts don't have a good reason. Removing pornography from the reach of children at convenience stores, for example, is a good cause. But I do think sometimes the method hasn't been helpful.

In the short-term, the boycott may hurt a company's business or result in a change of direction, but I wonder if it hurts the cause of Christians in the end. It seems, Joe, that Kinnaman might be right. We Christians are known more for what we are against than what we are for. We aren't known by our efforts to end the AIDS crisis or feed the hungry as much as we are for our campaign against Disney. We aren't known by our efforts to help people in our inner cities get out of poverty as much as we are for our campaign against Ford.

And Joe, I'm really hoping that will change.

-Tim

David Kinnaman says, "We have become famous for what we oppose, rather than who we are for."[1] Isn't that true much too often? The cable news networks love to pit two religious leaders against each other, and it angers me to watch them argue their points. It never seems to come down to what they believe in, but what they think someone else is doing that is wrong.

Christians have a longstanding history of being against pop culture, which came to the forefront in 1977 with the formation of the American Family Association. Over the past three decades, they have led boycotts against 7-Eleven, American Airlines, Abercrombie and Fitch,* and even American Girl. They were joined by Jerry Falwell's *Moral Majority* during the 1980s, which was followed by the very public boycott of Disney by the Southern Baptist Convention that began in 1997 and ended in 2005.

Even more recently with the release of *The Golden Compass* in December 2007, Christians made headlines by standing against this children's movie for its perceived atheistic message. Over 955 news articles were written about the response of Christians to this movie, with headlines such as "Christian Group Protests *The Golden Compass*" and "Church Warns Fantasy Film Is Anti-Religion" and "Religious Groups Call For Boycott of *The Golden Compass.*"

It seems as if every week I receive an opportunity by e-mail to boycott this, petition that, sign a covenant, or let a business know my Christian beliefs about its product. Honestly, these types of activities make me sick. Those businesses and organizations we want to boycott are being run and led by people—human beings—with families and kids and lives and choices. We may as well say to them, "Go to hell because I don't give a rip about your eternity. Just stay away from

---

* A member of my review team told me this story: "My wife worked at Abercrombie as a corporate trainer when the boycott was launched against the company. The majority of the employees were not followers of Christ and were completely turned off to Jesus because of the boycott. She was picking up the pieces for several years after that."

me and my family and out of our picket-fence-protected homes." Our actions are perceived as *holier than thou*, and they put us in the category of "all Christians are the same."

When did we decide the church should dictate, control, or mandate the direction of our culture? Isn't culture just a reflection of who we are as a society? Why are we focused on the fruit rather than the root? It would be like smashing all the apples from a tree in anger because they aren't big enough or tasty enough rather than considering the soil, sunlight, and environmental conditions; getting mad at the food when we should really be talking to the cook; or blaming the kids when we should talk to the parents.

Christians even use the Bible as a hammer against society hopefully to force it to reform. We think those who do not follow Jesus should act like those who do.

In their book *A Matrix of Meanings*, Detweiler and Taylor make a great point:

> In the New Testament, only the Gospels were written with the general public in mind. Yet many in the church read pop culture in light of Peter, Paul, and John's letters. Books of the Bible intended as "in-house" documents, designed to purify God's people, have been used inappropriately to correct the broader culture. So the warnings against sexual immorality in 1 Corinthians 7 get directed toward audiences Paul never intended.[2]

The authors go on to point out Paul's writing in 1 Corinthians 5:12–13, "What business is it of mine to judge those outside the church? Are you not to judge those inside? God will judge those outside."

I like how the same passage reads in *The Message:** "God decides on the outsiders, but we need to decide when our brothers and sisters are out of line and, if necessary, clean house."

Yet time and again, those who call themselves Christians, and many who are pastors or religious leaders, condemn the culture and reinforce the stereotype that all Christians are judgmental and unloving. It is no wonder that people such as Jeff, a twenty-five-year-old who doesn't go to church, was quoted in *unChristian* saying, "Christians talk about hating sin and loving sinners, but the way they go about things, they might as well call it what it is. They hate the sin and the sinner."[3]

SEPARATE FROM THE CULTURE

Meanwhile, across town at Cornerstone Community, Rev. Diebers began a series of messages on biblical separation. He was aware of all the ruckus in town about the movie production and wanted to make sure his congregation was prepared. He had taught them over the years about staying pure and fleeing from immorality, so he was confident that not many were in the habit of watching R-rated movies. But he knew they might be tempted to give in to the pressure to watch this movie upon its completion. Since it had been filmed in a familiar location, he knew the desire would be stronger than ever. So this new series would be a good opportunity to review the principles of being "in the world but not of the world."

I was about eight years old when a guest speaker came to our church. He was appropriately named Sketch Erickson, because he was also a sketch artist. As he spoke, he would draw pictures with chalk, and I can still vividly picture one in my mind. The title was, "Don't Let

---

* Some are opposed to quotes from *The Message*. It should be noted that Eugene Peterson's knowledge of Greek and Hebrew is deep and seasoned, making *The Message* extremely faithful to the original text.

the World Squeeze You Into Its Mold," and it had a picture of a guy all wrapped up inside a globe.

For years, I tried to live by that motto and follow all the rules. I truly wanted to stay away from anything in the world that would taint my soul. Yes, that is a good thing, but I think I went about it the wrong way because I never had to think for myself about what those things were—the lists were readily provided. At various times, the list included any music with drums, singers that held their own microphones or wore flashy jewelry while singing, jeans, denim of any kind, jewelry on men, swimming with the opposite sex (called "mixed bathing" for some reason), hair on guys that was too long, hair on girls that was too short, movie theaters, any video with higher than a PG-rating, drinking, smoking, chewing, pornography, the J. C. Penney catalog lingerie section, guys who wore hats in church, girls who didn't wear hats in church, dresses that didn't go below the knee, and on and on and on.

> **Following the rules is hard work. Just about the time I figured out what was on the list, I learned about a new list.**

Following the rules is hard work. Just about the time I figured out what was on the list, I learned about a new list. As an adult I worked at one Christian organization where no one was allowed to listen to any music—even personally, with headphones, on your own time—that had not been approved by the leaders. So we would turn in all our CDs and wait to find out what was approved and what had to be shelved.

It is interesting to me that Jesus didn't make many lists of things not to do; he focused more on lists of character qualities to embody. Some of his harshest criticism was against the religious leaders and their endless lists of dos and don'ts.

Matthew 12 tells the story of Jesus walking through a field with his disciples. The guys were hungry and they were grabbing some grain to munch on to hold them over until the next meal. The Pharisees saw this and went postal. "Your disciples are breaking the Sabbath rules!" they yelled at Jesus.

Jesus replied calmly, "Really? Didn't you ever read what David and his companions did when they were hungry, how they entered the sanctuary and ate fresh bread off the altar, bread that no one but priests were allowed to eat? And didn't you ever read in God's law that priests carrying out their temple duties break Sabbath rules all the time and it's not held against them?"

Good answer, Jesus. But he wasn't done. "There is far more at stake here than religion. If you had any idea what this scripture meant—'I prefer a flexible heart to an inflexible ritual'—you wouldn't be nitpicking like this. The Son of Man is no lackey to the Sabbath; he's in charge."[4]

If I had been one of Jesus' disciples, I would have been hiding behind a row of grain giving my buddies a high-five. What a great answer!

Jesus often communicated that it's not primarily about what you do or don't do. It is not about lists. It is about your heart. It is about being right with God.[*]

I think the entire Sermon on the Mount could arguably be for the purpose of minimizing our reliance on lists and focusing instead on the condition of our hearts. Jesus said, "You don't murder? So what? What's in your heart toward that person?" He said, "You haven't committed adultery? So what? Your heart can be corrupted by lust even faster than your body." It was a heart issue.

Many things in the Bible are black and white; they are indisputably wrong, such as having sex with your friend's wife. However, is an

---

[*] Matthew 23 contains an entire message by Jesus against the rules of the Pharisees.

R-rated movie wrong to see? Is it wrong for a Christian to watch *Desperate Housewives*? Should you listen to a song that contains profanity? I don't know. Maybe for you it is okay. Maybe for me it is sin.[*] What's in your heart? Where does that activity take your mind?

Here is what I know. It made Jesus very angry when the religious leaders of his day made rules that were not in the Bible and imposed them on everyone else. Jesus called the religious leaders who obeyed every one of more than six hundred laws "a brood of vipers"[5] because of their unclean hearts. Another way to say this is they had "minds like a snake pit." I don't know about you, but I'd rather Jesus not know me as having a dirty heart or snake-infested mind.

EMBRACE THE CULTURE

Taking the opposite view from either Grace Church or Cornerstone Community was what Bob Franklin did. He was the presiding pastor at Glenmoor Central, an established congregation that was known for its progressive views. Their slogan the entire year, since Pastor Franklin had arrived in town, was "Open Arms," and it had been rumored that they rarely ever preached out of the Bible. With all the excitement about the famous celebrities coming to town, Bob decided to open the gates wide and do whatever it would take to build a huge crowd during the weeks the cast members were in town.

He started by contacting a friend in Los Angeles who knew someone who knew someone else who had a connection to one of the producers of the movie filming in Glenmoor. His assignment to his friend: "Get me anyone you can to speak at my church. I want a different actor every week of the summer if possible!"

"I'll check," his friend replied. "What type of speaker are you looking for? Any particular topic? Does he have to be a Christian?"

"None of that matters. Just having an individual from the cast at the church will build a huge crowd. We can figure out later what we'll talk about. If they

---

* I'm not talking about a Gospel of relativism. The Bible is our final authority, but Romans 14 clearly indicates there might be activities that are okay for one Christian and wrong for another.

aren't comfortable speaking, I can even interview them. We'll find a topic that is comfortable to them."

There is a mindless embracing of the culture that is worrisome to me. Too many leaders check their brains and their hearts at the door and run after whatever is cool, whatever is trendy, whatever will bring in a bigger crowd.

Don't get me wrong. I am a numbers guy. Numbers represent people and the more numbers (i.e. people) we can get in the front door, the better. Steven Furtick, a pastor in North Carolina, probably said it even better: "If you get the impression that we're all about the numbers, let me clarify. Of course we're all about the numbers. What else would we be all about? The spaghetti supper? To hell with the spaghetti supper. I want to see some changed lives!"[6]

The problem comes with our motivation. Some take the posture that *the end justifies the means* and have no boundaries for what they will do to build a crowd. If it means watering down the message, they will do it. If it means giving out free beer or showing the entire R-rated movie in the service or celebrating the sinful activity that happens within the film—it doesn't matter. If it builds a crowd, then it is fair game.

I think it is crucial that we don't lose the message in the method. At Granger, we are criticized all the time for our methods, but I have never once heard someone (who actually attended a service) say we are soft on the message.

Craig Groeschel, pastor of LifeChurch.tv (named the most innovative church in America by *Outreach Magazine* in 2007 and 2008[7]), says he thinks the "pendulum has swung too far. Now, in some places, church is so relevant that we almost seem to worship culture more than Christ."[8]

It would sadden me if the result of this book were an abandonment of scripture in favor of being more culturally relevant. Groeschel says that having cool lights, awesome video, a coffee shop, and a sermon series with catchy titles isn't bad, but "when people *do* finally come to church, we should help them experience Christ—not just something that looks like a rock concert, coffee bar, or movie theater." I could not agree more.

IGNORE THE CULTURE

Pastor Melissa Ellsworth had been at First Church since the economic boom of the early 1980s. She was old enough and wise enough not to be swayed by the daily headlines. For more than twenty years, she had pastored this small flock, and they counted on her to encourage and inspire them. It was her practice to keep teaching the Word, regardless of what was happening around them. So for the entire year, she just kept working through her series on the book of Ruth. She never mentioned the movie production, not even in a prayer. Several of her parishioners thanked her for helping them find a haven away from the insanity that was outside those walls.

The catastrophe on 9/11 happened on a Tuesday morning, and within a few days almost every church in America was deciding what to do that weekend. At Granger, we were two weeks into a five-week series called "Extreme Success." We were exploring biblical truths that could help you in your daily life at work. We had invested several thousand dollars on a stage set that had a painted backdrop with skyscrapers (thus the "success" analogy) and in front of the skyscrapers were

> **Not even in their opening or closing prayer did they acknowledge the events of the previous week.**

various dummies dressed in business attire performing stunts (thus the "extreme" analogy). One guy was hanging upside down riding a skateboard. Another was riding a dirt bike.

As soon as 9/11 happened, having bodies hanging upside down in front of skyscrapers took on an entirely new meaning. We made an easy decision—the entire set had to be scrapped. The community wasn't thinking about how to do better in their jobs. Everyone was thinking about his or her safety and the future of the country. Where was God in all this? What is an Islamic fundamentalist?

Another church in the Chicago area had a very different response. One of our staff members was there visiting a family member and was shocked to discover how they responded.

This church went on as if nothing at all had happened. It was the week of their annual Hispanic Appreciation Sunday, and they saw no need to change that. Although attendance was up because of the tragedy on everyone's mind, the church went on as though it were a normal Sunday. Not even in their opening or closing prayer did they acknowledge the events of the previous week.

I didn't talk to the pastor, but I am guessing it was an intentional decision. He probably believed the church should be a haven. I'm sure he thought, "Our people have been watching this on the news 24/7 since Tuesday—I'm going to give them something else to think about."

What a mistake! What an opportunity lost! On the day when more people in the country were in tune to their spiritual journeys and eternal destinies than ever, this church totally ignored it.

Many churches do this every week of the year. Events are happening in the culture around them, and rather than seize the opportunity to talk about it and help people make sense of the spiritual realities woven through the fabric of their lives, they ignore it.

A hugely successful book and subsequent movie such as *The DaVinci Code* comes out and soon one out of every three adults has been exposed to it. They have new questions about their faith, about Jesus, and about the trustworthiness of the Bible, and some churches completely ignore it.

A blockbuster movie such as *Spider-Man 3* premieres that is full of spiritual topics. What an opportunity to talk about forgiveness, regret, destiny, and choices. Suddenly, a common language can be used, if only for a short window of time, that will connect to a larger group of people than attend on a typical Sunday. But some churches intentionally ignore the opportunity, not wanting to risk offending the regulars.

And so the world passes by, never hearing how much they matter to God.

LEVERAGE THE CULTURE

John Bixby had only been the pastor at River Pointe Church for a couple of years. In his short tenure, he had helped them discover why they exist as a church, walked them delicately through a change to their name that better reflected the mission of the church, and helped them begin to rediscover their purpose to reach out to the community. This process led them to the conclusion to scrap their relocation plans. Instead, they intentionally decided to stay in the neighborhood where they believed they had the greatest chance of making a difference.

Soon after the mayor had shared the big news about the filming of a Tom Cruise movie, John called his leadership team together to discuss the potential this could have. After two years of leading and training this group, John sat back and watched his team respond with love and grace—he couldn't have been more proud. One of the elders led the conversation by saying, "There are going to be six hundred people here from Hollywood who need to know how much they matter to God!"

The leader of the men's prayer breakfast jumped in and said, "I'm not excited about the theme of the movie—God knows it's already hard enough to keep my kids safe. But that's not the point. The entire community is going to be watching how the church responds. Are we going to point our finger at them with judgment? Or are we going to accept them right where they are?"

Marge Hudson, an elderly parishioner who had been at the church since before John was born, said, "Those crew members are going to be hot and hungry—maybe we should do something about that." And with those words, a plan was born. Teams of volunteers from the church began to give out cold bottles of water to the crew each afternoon in what would later be determined the hottest summer on record. Each morning they distributed newspapers—not the local Glenmoor Daily. No, they had arranged to get a supply of the LA Times each day so the cast members had a little feeling of home.

How can we leverage the culture to reach as many people as we possibly can without compromising our biblical message?

It also became quickly evident there wouldn't be enough hotel rooms in town to accommodate the influx of people, so after a few phone calls River Pointe Church became the official clearinghouse to find homes in the community that had extra bedrooms. They then coached these host families to just love, accept, and listen—and not preach.

John then planned a series of messages to help make a positive connection to the culture. He didn't want to use the themes from the movie that was being filmed in Glenmoor, but he found five other movies in which Tom Cruise had starred and used one each week to introduce a biblical theme. He called the series "Cruise Control: Letting God Take the Wheel" (which his fourteen-year-old daughter immediately told him was the cheesiest thing she'd ever heard and would be horrified if she ran into Tom Cruise in the grocery store).

I didn't attend the pretend meeting at this made-up church, but here are some questions I have to believe they were considering:

How can we leverage the culture to reach as many people as we possibly can without compromising our biblical message? How can we maximize an opportunity we may never have again to share the love of God with six hundred people who will be living in our town for three months? How can we show our community how much they matter to God without them thinking we want anything in return?

How can we use this to help us impact some of our friends and neighbors who have never shown a previous interest in attending church? What are some topics we can address from the Bible that will really help people at their biggest point of need?

In a sense, they were seeing an opportunity to engage the culture. They weren't changing their mission. They had no plan to soften the message or exclude certain parts because unbelievers would find them hard to swallow. They were just seeing an opportunity and choosing to leverage that in order to reach more people.

PULLING IT ALL TOGETHER

Five churches. Five leaders. Five vastly different responses. All of them aware of a major pop culture event having an impact on everyone in their community. Yet, each made a different choice on how to respond.

I'm not sure they all made a conscious choice. For some of them, they responded as naturally as they would if they saw a child fall off a bike. Instinct kicks in. Training pays off. Experience guides. A choice is made.

And it is the same set of choices every church has about how to deal with the ever-pervasive pop culture that surrounds our congregations.

Five choices.

Grace Church (interesting name, huh?) chose to **condemn** the culture. Let the world know what is wrong. Reject those who align themselves with the sin of the culture.

Cornerstone Community chose the route of **separation**. Say nothing to the public, but make sure our congregation knows to avoid the sin and the sinners.

Glenmoor Central looked straight at the culture and gave it a full frontal hug. **Embrace** the culture. No discernment. No filter. The goal was more people. We will figure everything else out later.

First Church just went on doing church as usual. People have enough clutter in their minds and lives. **Ignore** the culture. Let's just stay focused on the Word of God and provide inspirational services.

River Pointe looked for new and creative ways to let people know how much they matter to God. Let's **leverage** this pop culture event so we can reach as many people as we possibly can.

Condemn. Separate. Embrace. Ignore. Leverage.

I hope you will choose to leverage. I think you will after you see how full of hope the culture around you is. More about that in the next chapter.

chapter 5

LINKIN PARK SINGS.
GOD SPEAKS.

The invention of the arts, and other things which serve the common use and convenience of life, is a gift of God by no means to be despised, and a faculty worthy of commendation.

—John Calvin, Commentary on Genesis

What an amazing time to be alive! Have you considered the miraculous age in which we live?

Through the incredible invention of flight, we live in a time when you can be standing in your living room in Georgia today and walking through a village in India tomorrow. While driving I-5 in Los Angeles, you can be talking on a phone to someone who is cruising on the autobahn in Germany, thousands of miles away, without a cord to connect you. You can flip on your television in North Dakota and watch live video coming from the war in Iraq—seeing the action on the frontlines as it is happening. You can be sitting on your couch killing bad guys in *Halo 3*, along with members of your team who are sitting on their own couches in Sweden, Zimbabwe, Canada, and Brazil.

Never before in human history have we had the benefit of the innovations and technologies that exist here early in the twenty-first century. We have access from our homes to virtually every piece of information available to humankind. In fact, Google announced in 2005 its intent to digitize every book ever printed in every language, and they want to give you access to all of it from your home computer. They already have over one million books scanned and are adding more than three thousand books a day to their collection.[1] Additionally, most homes have more than one personal computer sitting on a desk, capable of processing data and storing information that would have taken several room-sized mainframe computers just three decades ago.

Perhaps the amazing world we live in is no better illustrated than in the world of medicine. Illnesses that would have killed you just a few years ago are now curable. Doctors can perform minimally invasive surgeries through advancements in laser technology, and you can go home after surgery and return to work the following day. Do you have an irreversible eye disease? No problem—an ophthalmologist can replace your cornea. Do you have a bad heart? Options exist for surgery, transplants, and even inserting an artificial heart.

Doctors today can give you a vaccine for hepatitis B, rubella, mumps, measles, polio, yellow fever, tetanus, tuberculosis and more. Not one of these vaccines existed one hundred years ago. As a result, life expectancy, which was only forty-seven years in 1900, has increased to more than seventy-five years in North America. In addition, advancements in sewage treatment and water filtration are increasing life expectancy around the world. It is possible we will see the large-scale alleviation of poverty and preventable diseases in underdeveloped countries within our lifetimes.

In the past century, the medical advancements have been astounding. The technological inventions have changed the face of the earth. Recent scientific discoveries and engineering innovations have revolutionized our ability to survive and greatly enhance our quality of life. It is unbelievable.

Just as amazing as all that is the explosion we have seen in the arts. One hundred years ago, your options for celebrating or participating in the arts were likely limited to a stage production, an art museum, a symphony, or an issue of the *Saturday Evening Post*. Just fifty years ago, there were only a few musical genres, three television stations, and no internet—but so much has changed since then.

In today's world, we have at our disposal well over five hundred television stations, hundreds of musical genres,[2] millions of books, and billions of internet pages. In addition, live productions have made a comeback with groups such as Cirque du Soleil, Blue Man

Group, and Stomp leading the way. And the world of video games is now a $50 billion industry. The creative arts are bursting with variety, volume, and excellence as never before.

As I observe a sampling of the contemporary work of millions of artists around the world—in media, music, fashion, art, photography, writing, architecture, acting and more—I can't help but celebrate. I see the work of the artist, and regardless of whether their intent was God honoring, it points me to their Creator. I experience a moment of pure artistic genius, and it gives me a feeling, a sense of how awesome and majestic our God is. I experience the same feeling standing at the base of an eighty-story skyscraper as I do when I stare at the vastness of the ocean—both point me to a God who thought the ocean into existence and created the architect of the skyscraper with his own hands.

So we can celebrate the art—knowing it came from the skills, intelligence, and creativity of a being fashioned by God himself. We can also celebrate the content of much of the art in the world today—art that reflects a real search and longing for that which is right and true. Like Paul speaking to the Athenians,[3] we can say, "I see you are seeking God. Let me tell you more about this God you seek."

ALL TRUTH IS GOD'S TRUTH

These days it is popular to be connected to Jesus. From the commercialism of *WWJD* merchandise to the reality that everyone in the world, it seems, wears a cross around his or her neck, it is hip to have a connection to Jesus. However, this is not what excites me. In fact, I think much of what is available in the Christian market is cheesy and lacks authenticity. I resonate with the words of Steve Stockman who said, "We have created a vast industry that, as well as making Christian businessmen bucket loads of money, has also isolated the Christian faith."[4]

What does make my heart beat fast, however, is to see how God is alive and well in today's pop culture. You cannot turn on the TV, listen to the radio, watch a movie, or browse the shelves for a best-seller without seeing evidence of God speaking through our culture.

> I think much of what is available in the Christian market is cheesy and lacks authenticity.

The Bible is clear that all truth is God's truth, regardless of the source. In fact, when the Pharisees were trying to get Jesus to tell his disciples to shut up (they wouldn't stop praising him), Jesus answers, "If they keep quiet, the stones will cry out!"[5] Truth is going to be revealed, whether or not it is coming from the mouth of a Christian. Stockman says, "Sometimes we find the truth where we have been told it shouldn't belong, eternal truth in the seemingly most unlikely music."[6]

I can identify with this so much. There have been times when the words of a song verbalized what I was feeling and spoke truth to me. I remember the first time I heard the band Linkin Park sing "Numb" and felt the words echo my own struggle with God. With the song-writer, I was crying, *"I've become so numb I can't feel you there. I'm tired of being what you want me to be."*[7] Their words remind me of the cry of Jeremiah: *"These are bad times for me! It's one thing after another. God is piling on the pain. I'm worn out and there's no end in sight."*[8]

At a time when I was experiencing deep pain in a relationship, another Linkin Park song, "Easier to Run," helped me face my own selfish desires: *"It's easier to run, replacing this pain with something numb. It's so much easier to go than face all this pain here all alone."*[9]

Sometimes the truth comes through a TV show. As my teen girls are getting older, I find myself tuned in to culture in new ways. On the CBS show *Shark,* I find myself identifying with the character

Sebastian Stark as he tries to relate to his daughter Julie. God has used this show to help me realize, again, the importance of my relationship with Heather and Megan during these formative years in their lives. Sebastian is a hero at his office—but misses so many opportunities that only come through quantity* time with his daughter.

In an episode of *Desperate Housewives,*[10] Gabrielle (the supermodel) is obviously very uncomfortable sitting with Lynette during her chemo treatments. She finally breaks down weeping and talks about her memories of sitting with her father as he died. She was five years old at the time, and instructed by her mom never to stop smiling. She

Joe,

I expect you are much better at this than we who spend a lot of time in church are. Looking for truth in the culture is a skill we've never been taught. For you, life is much more integrated. Since you don't go to church, you aren't accustomed to isolating your spirituality to a certain day in the week. When you watch a TV show and as a result are motivated to give something away or do something kind, you see it as a step in your faith.

Don't lose that. If you do start going to church every week, don't let the church bubble cause your insight to be lost. Seeing God in culture is no different from seeing God in nature. In either instance, you can rush right through going from here to there and forget to pay attention to the beauty and truth that is all around.

-Tim

---

* This isn't a typo. You may think quality time is more important than quantity time. But you never know when those few minutes of quality time are going to happen. The only way to ensure that you will have good quality time with your kids is by spending large amounts of quantity time with them.

confesses to Lynette, "I've made a career out of smiling on the outside when I'm dying on the inside." Through the episode, the damaging consequences of a life of lies are clearly shown.

If you are like me, perhaps you are sometimes surprised that God is speaking to you so strongly through the culture. Stockman says it is because we are not looking for God in the culture. In fact, we have been taught not to look. He says, "We are convinced it is wrong to look. There is a bizarre arrogance that pervades many Christian circles that truth is confined to those who have a seamless profession of faith." For some reason, we think that if a professing Christian says something that is true—then it is valid. If a *worldly* artist speaks the same words, they are not valid.

I don't think I have ever heard this verbalized better than in the book *Matrix of Meanings*:

> We believe popular music should be heard in the
> same manner as the Psalms, as celebrations of the
> gift of God-given life. But the Top 40 charts also
> contain songs of longing, regret, anger, and doubt.
> Pop music has helped us hear the Psalms as prayers,
> formed in frustration, offered to a sometimes hidden
> God. We appreciate Job's sufferings even more after
> watching Mel Gibson's struggle in *Signs*. Proverbs'
> recurring emphasis on the danger of shortcuts, the
> snares of temptation, and the rewards of honesty
> finds expression in sitcoms such as *The Simpsons*.
> The Song of Solomon's obsession with love, with
> the celebration of the physical, dominates the radio
> dial. The weariness expressed in Ecclesiastes flows
> through the precincts of *NYPD Blue* and the suburbs
> of *American Beauty*. Lamentations deals with grief,

which Eric Clapton captured so eloquently in "Tears in Heaven."[11]

SACRED VS. SECULAR

It seems that some in the Christian world try so desperately to categorize everything as to whether it is Christian or secular. And so we have categories called Christian music, Christian fiction, Christian magazines, and even Christian artwork. You can take a Christian cruise, invest in Christian stocks, fill your time viewing Christian television, and tune into GodTube instead of YouTube. We don't want our kids trick-or-treating with the world so we schedule a Christian activity for the kids at church on Halloween. We don't want to be exposed to cussing and innuendos, so instead of joining the city sports teams, we form our own Christian leagues. And to keep our kids away from society, we send them to a Christian school with Christian teachers and Christian friends so they can learn the Christian way to read, write, and add.

Two things happen when we do this. First, we remove our influence from the world. Instead of working to bring God's kingdom here on earth or focusing on being salt and light in a dark world, we spend our time intent on making sure none of the dirt of the world gets on us. In effect, we exclude ourselves from the world. Like in the movie *The Village* by M. Night Shyamalan, we build a fence around our lives and do everything within our Christian community. The world outside can go to hell as far as we are concerned. We have our ticket to heaven and don't want to be pulled down by someone who doesn't.

The second thing that happens when we try to make our entire lives *Christian* is that we fail to teach our kids (or learn ourselves) how to be discerning. The mental muscle that helps us filter our response to what is good and bad is never exercised. So when we do interact with someone outside our Christian bubble, we come off as fanatical

90

WHAT ABOUT THE KIDS?

You might be wondering, "Do you allow your kids to watch anything they want?" Absolutely not. We don't allow them to surf channels, we monitor their music, and we have software protecting them from the dangers on the internet. So am I talking out of both sides of my mouth?

I don't think so. The goal of my wife and me is to raise kids who meet Jesus and fully integrate their faith into the culture in which they live. That is a process that won't be complete until they have  left our home. As parents of small children, we monitor everything very closely. We don't even allow them to watch TV commercials. Their little minds are too moldable. Watching commercials can make them discontent and materialistic. Mainstream music can make them focused on outward appearances. Some TV shows and movies can desensitize them to violence or introduce them to concepts they don't need to know about yet.

As they get older, we begin to let the leash out. We are there all along the way to help them develop their *discernment muscle*. I remember taking my young girls (probably six and seven years old at the time) to see *Remember the Titans*. It was only rated PG but had some very adult themes. We talked after the movie about racism and about why some people are mean to others. Now they are young teenagers, and they are beginning to get more freedom to pick their own music, watch some shows with Mom and Dad, and have fewer restrictions on the internet. But all the time we are watching and talking, helping them learn how to find God in the medium and make choices that would honor him. Watching movies or TV shows with some adult storylines together with our girls has created some special moments of quality conversation and is helping mold them into young women who have a fully integrated walk with Jesus.

or weird—worse yet, as superior and judgmental.

None of these *Christian* things or activities is wrong. I'm glad my teen daughters listen to the local Christian radio station. I grew up in a Christian school, and I am so grateful for the sacrifice my parents made to make that possible. I even subscribe to some Christian magazines. I am not suggesting that you should avoid something with a *Christian* tag on it.

Where I believe we should exercise caution is in having black and white categories for what is secular and what is sacred. Madeleine L'Engle, in her book, *Walking on Water*, says, "To look at a work of art and then to make a judgment as to whether or not it is Christian is presumptuous. It is something we cannot know in any conclusive way. We can know only if it speaks within our own hearts and leads us to living more deeply with Christ in God."[12]

Steve Beard, founder and author of Thunderstruck.org, experienced this when he went to a U2 concert during their *Elevation* tour. Steve says of his experience,

> I was amazed at how often I felt the presence of God in the arena. God used the opportunity to speak to me throughout the night. Not being a well-attuned mystic, I was rather surprised. The culmination of the evening was the final encore. After thanking "the Almighty" numerous times, Bono began singing "hallelujah" over and over and over again. This rather contagious melody and message rang throughout the audience's soul. Soon, it seemed as though all sixteen thousand fans in the arena were singing the song with Bono. This one word: Hallelujah—praise ye the Lord. With that, they walked off the stage.[13]

Instead of trying to categorize art as to whether it is sacred or secular, good or evil, positive or negative—let's engage the culture in a conversation. Let's celebrate the truth wherever we encounter it. Let's applaud people when we see they are on a journey toward God, even if somewhat misguided. Let's leverage popular art to connect to our communities in ways they can understand. Let's work hard to uncover the positive and not so hard on exposing the negative. After all, Craig Detweiler says, "It is easy to identify what's wrong with Eminem, but finding what's right, identifying and understanding what millions of teens connect with, takes much more work."[14]

To make that work a little easier, let's break it down...

chapter 6

FINDING GOD IN POP CULTURE IS EASIER THAN YOU THINK

Given the power of media, becoming conversant with its mixed messages is an essential tool for the Christian life. This involves the process of inculturation—discovering where Christ is already active within a given culture…The risen Christ sends us out to our media-saturated culture…and in it we labor with Christ to expose the signs of God's saving love already present there. We cannot speak to a culture we do not know or one we despise…We have to learn its language and discover how Christ has already gone ahead of us, inculturated in some of media's values, stories, and style.

—Richard Leonard

In *Matrix of Meanings,* the authors tell us, "If you look close enough, beyond the surface provocations, you will see that pop culture reflects a longing for authentic truth, beauty, freedom, and love. Can we put our ears to the ground and find the current rhythms with which to reach even the most skeptical viewer?"[1] I think we can.

While the list that follows is not exhaustive, I would like to consider seven themes about which the culture is already talking. They are writing songs, creating movies, and broadcasting TV shows on and around these seven topics and often including the eternal truths of God in their art, whether they know it or not.* We have a great opportunity to tune in and engage our communities in conversation and even leverage the culture to increase our impact through the local church. The seven themes are:

1. A fascination with eternity and the supernatural
2. A longing for relationships
3. Love and sex
4. Honesty and authenticity

* I am only exploring music, shows, and movies, but there are also many examples that could be cited in each of these categories of video games, magazines, stage productions, and bestsellers.

5. A desire for purpose
6. Bitterness and revenge
7. Justice and redemption

As I unpack each of these themes below, I realize that by giving examples of specific artists, shows, or movies, this chapter will become dated even before it is published. Because I am writing this in early 2008, many of the examples I cite may be well off your radar by the time you read this. However, I encourage you to come up with your own list and determine how you can engage your community in these areas where the culture already has an interest. Whether you are reading this in 2008 or in 2018, I believe these categories will be explored through our popular culture for years to come. You can also visit PopGoesTheChurch.com for examples that are more recent.💻⁾

A FASCINATION WITH ETERNITY AND THE SUPERNATURAL

Popular artists have found a thousand ways to talk about death and the afterlife and to depict God and the supernatural. From an older movie such as *It's a Wonderful Life* (1946) to newer movies such as *City of Angels* (1998) and *Bruce Almighty* (2003), God and angelic beings have long been sources of entertainment. Songwriters have been fascinated by the topic also, with hits including "Where the Streets Have No Name" by U2 and "Heaven" by the Los Lonely Boys.

A fascination with good, evil, and the afterlife has also been a winner on primetime year after year, and the shows that debuted in the fall of 2007 were no different. New shows such as *Reaper*, *Pushing Daisies*, and *Moonlight* all delve into the supernatural. This fascination with death and what comes later seems to indicate an awareness of our mortality. Even in Hollywood with the money for Botox and

💻⁾ KEYWORD: SEVEN | PopGoesTheChurch.com

microscopic lasers to extend youth (or at least mask aging), there still is this impending, ever-closer reality called death that no one has been able to avert. This dialogue may start in Hollywood, but they bring it to the forefront of the cultural conversation in every community, and soon our friends and neighbors are considering the possibility and ramifications of life after death. The culture is ripe for the church to address the here and now and the choices we make that have an impact in the afterlife.

This fascination with the afterlife is not a Hollywood phenomenon—it is an eternal truth of God. The New Testament tells us "these sterile and barren bodies of ours are yearning for full deliverance."[2] The popular culture is just illustrating it for us.

Equally capturing the creativity of Hollywood is the supernatural. A drama debuted on TNT in the summer of 2007 called *Saving Grace* starring Holly Hunter. It was a raw and gritty view of a woman on a spiritual search and her encounter with the supernatural. One of the few primetime shows with a TV-MA rating, it contained nudity, profanity, adultery, and violence and definitely deserved its adult rating.

TV Guide best summarized the plot:

> Hunter plays Grace Hanadarko, an Oklahoma City police detective who seems to break as many rules as she enforces. She drinks...to excess. She's an exhibitionist. She's adulterous. And on one fateful night, in the first episode, a confluence of her myriad trespasses finds her racing along a seemingly desolate road until she mows down an innocent pedestrian. It is then that she is afforded a most unlikely second chance, in the form of an atypical angelic figure named Earl. The lady cop, though, is not immediately ready to tone down her hard-living ways...[3]

I found so much to be learned from this show. There are hundreds of people like Grace all around us. Like so many, she is self-sufficient and has no need for God, but she has this gnawing ache for purpose and a sense that *there must be more to life than this.* She doesn't make her decisions based on a foundation of morality. Without that, who cares if the guy you are sleeping with is married? Without being grounded in what is right or wrong, who cares if you bend rules to get to a preferred outcome?

Grace's brother is a Catholic priest who has no idea how to handle his sister. He comes across as intolerant and judgmental. I wonder, though, if it is a good picture of how many of us come across to people like Grace. In addition, Earl is not who you ever pictured as an angel. He has long hair, is overweight, and chews tobacco, yet in his attitude and treatment of Grace, he displays a balance between the God-like nature of love and holiness. That will mess with your image of the divine.

A LONGING FOR RELATIONSHIPS

In all forms of pop culture, we also see a longing for relationships portrayed, and so it should be, as it is a very part of our DNA. It is clear that we have been created by God to be in relationship with him and with others. Although the Trinity is a tough concept to understand, we know he is hardwired for relationship, and that we were made in his image. What is easier to understand, yet still difficult to integrate into our lives, are the words of Jesus when he was asked to boil all of scripture down to its irreducible minimum. He said it comes down to two relationships: love God and love others.[4]

> **It is clear that we have been created by God to be in relationship with him and with others.**

This desire for a meaningful relationship with someone else has been depicted in Hollywood many times, but perhaps one of the classic films was *Pretty Woman* in 1990. Edward Lewis, played by Richard Gere, is trying to fill a void in his relational life by hiring a prostitute, and Vivian Ward, played by Julia Roberts, is broken and rejected and wanting to experience true acceptance for the first time in her life. Both of them are pursuing a connection with the other, and you can almost experience their feelings as they are hoping the other will be able to satisfy their inner desires.

There have been scores of TV shows that are entirely about relationships, including *Friends, Desperate Housewives,* and *Grey's Anatomy.* One of my favorites that explores the depths of relationships is *Friday Night Lights.* In a November 2007 episode, Tim Riggins, an alcoholic teen who is trying to figure life out, travels with his crippled friend, Jason Street, to Mexico to find an alternative treatment for his paralysis. While there, he calls Lyla Garrity, Jason's ex-girlfriend and a very outspoken Christian, and asks her to come to Mexico to talk Jason out of the risky surgery. Lyla travels down, but gets frustrated by their frivolity and drinking and wants nothing of it. She threatens to leave. In an emotional showdown, Tim Riggins says, "I may be as screwed up as you think I am, but at least I'm by Jason's side. You, you're ready to jump on the next plane back to Texas. At least I'm going through whatever it is we're gonna go through together. I sin daily and I'm a better Christian than you."[5]

God used this comment by a fictional character on TV in my own life and kept me thinking for days about my own friendships and whether my Christianity is real enough to be the kind of friend to Jason that Tim was.

LOVE AND SEX

As a reminder, we are exploring areas of truth about which the culture is already talking. And no one would deny that love and sex get plenty of airtime in our popular culture. However, we sometimes forget that God created sex. It was his idea. Think about that for a few minutes. Let it sink in. For God so loved the world that he created sex. He designed the relationship between man and woman and gave us the ability to express our love to each other through the intimacy of sex in the context of a committed marriage relationship.

> **Even in the perversion of sex, you find the truth that we all want to be loved.**

So many songs have been written about the pursuit of love and sex through the years and about the distortion of those pursuits.

One of the most popular songs of 2007 was a sweet love song called "Hey There, Delilah" by the Plain White T's. It is the story of an amateur musician trying to make it big, writing a love song to his girl who is hundreds of miles away going to school. He is longing to be with her and promising that he would walk to her if he could find no other way. Ahhhh, that gives me warm fuzzies.

In the not-so-sweet column is "Irreplaceable" by Beyonce Knowles. In a moment of pain, she pretends that love is easy to find and sings, "Baby I won't shed a tear for you, I won't lose a wink of sleep, 'cause the truth of the matter is, replacing you is so easy." But it isn't that easy. In her hurt, she is masking her pain.

Hinder wrote of a forbidden love in "The Lips of an Angel" and acknowledged that she makes it "hard to be faithful." Yet he continues to pursue it and fan the flames of the affair.

Even in the perversion of sex, you find the truth that we all want to be loved. In the 2007 movie release of *Georgia Rule*, the dysfunctional relationships between a grandmother, mother, and daughter play out. In one scene, the teenage daughter, Rachel, offers to perform a sex act on Harlan, a local town boy. He lets her do it and then asks her why she did. She tearfully replies, "I was just looking for someone to say no." Wow! What a moment of sheer honesty. I wonder how many teens are in an unstructured environment of chaos and limitless freedom, continually tripped up by their choices, just wishing someone would say no.

In any sexual sin, there is a moment of choice that can lead one down the path toward destruction. I have never seen this portrayed more clearly than in the 2002 movie *Unfaithful* with Diane Lane and Richard Gere. On a windy day, a middle-aged woman falls in the street, scuffs up her knee, and drops her belongings. A younger man approaching his nearby apartment stops to help. She is grateful, and a little flattered, that he has taken notice of her. She looks around for a taxi, cannot seem to find one, and she is then invited up to his apartment to get cleaned up. She stops, thinks about it, looks down the street at an approaching taxi, and then intentionally decides to follow him up to his apartment.

That one choice led to an illicit affair, the destruction of her marriage, and eventually even a murder and a cover-up. Toward the end of the movie, they replay in slow motion the fateful choice—seemingly innocent at the time—of choosing to go into his apartment when she knew in her heart it was the wrong choice.

I think if every married couple watched this movie together, it would create space for conversation about their commitment to each other. They might reflect on boundaries that will protect their marriage from a bad choice made in a moment of weakness.

HONESTY AND AUTHENTICITY

Is there a character quality lacking more in today's world than honesty? Is there a foundational value that is more in demand than authenticity? In 2004, Tim McGraw released the hit "Live like You

Were Dying" and sang about a man who learns he doesn't have long to live. So what did he do? He said, "I loved deeper, and I spoke sweeter, and I gave forgiveness I'd been denyin', and he said some day I hope you get the chance to live like you were dyin'." He quit playing games and got real.

Michael Clayton (2007), starring George Clooney, was a movie that felt real and believable. The story was about several characters who had lived a lifetime of lies. In fact, one gentleman had lied for so long he just snapped. He could no longer keep up the façade. This movie really expressed the angst and hopelessness with which so many around us live and asked many significant questions: How long would you do something you knew was wrong even if it was very lucrative? What would you do for a family member who messed up but needed your help? When we are under stress, why do we ignore the relationships that mean the most to us? How long can you sell your soul for something less than what God made you to be?

A DESIRE FOR PURPOSE

What an important question—how long can you sell your soul for something less than what God made you to be? Finding purpose for living may be one of the most difficult searches that a man or woman goes through. A person can have money, love, a great job, and a loving family, but if he doesn't know why he was created it will drive him to do just about anything.

That search explains why the TV show *Heroes* quickly became a success upon its debut in the fall of 2006. It portrays a bunch of average people struggling through life who suddenly discover they possess extraordinary gifts. We all want to make a difference. For most people, it is a desire that exceeds wanting to make money or become famous. At Granger in October 2007, we offered a weekend series based on the show *Heroes* with this lead-in: "Have you ever had the

Joe,

Can you identify with what I'm saying? Have you ever felt like you were meant for something more? Have you looked at the problems of the world and wanted to make a difference? I want to encourage you to lean into that. That is something special, and it didn't just happen. God placed it in your heart.

That means the God of the universe cares so much about you that he created you on purpose and for a purpose. I hope you can see that. I hope you keep asking questions and searching for answers and trying to figure it out. When you feel something inside that pushes you to make a difference in someone else's life, it is God. So accept that God has a purpose for you and keep trying to figure it out.

I believe God will honor your search and help you find your purpose.

-Tim

feeling you were meant for something extraordinary?" Even those far from God have a desire for significance. Addressing that desire gives us an inroad to their hearts—a path to introduce them to Christ.

Leo Partible is an independent movie producer, graphic artist, and writer, and says, "People are looking for heroes. People are looking for answers to the big questions, like, 'What am I doing here?' I asked that question when I was a kid, and some of the comic books I read did a better job of answering it than many of the sermons I heard from preachers back then."[6]

In 2004, we all connected with the words of the well-known hit by Switchfoot, "We were meant to live for so much more, have we lost ourselves?" The Bible tells us "everything got started in him and finds its purpose in him."[7] It is an innate, God-given desire to want to know our purpose. What else can explain over twenty-five million copies of *The Purpose Driven Life* by Rick Warren being sold, making it the best-selling hardback book in history?

In October 2007, a whole slate of TV programming was introduced that picks up on the same theme of *normal* people finding their purpose and making an extraordinary difference. *Chuck* features a computer nerd that becomes a top American spy when all of the nation's secret intelligence is downloaded into his brain. A struggling writer suddenly becomes a hero as he travels back in time on *Journeyman*. And we can't forget to mention the remake of *Bionic Woman*, whose surgery gone awry gives her incredible superpowers and great responsibility.

BITTERNESS AND REVENGE

God tells us clearly not to take revenge,[8] but sometimes we are tempted to take things into our own hands. Carrie Underwood sings about this in "Before He Cheats." She decides to teach an unfaithful man a lesson he won't soon forget, and says, "I dug my key into the side of his pretty little souped-up four-wheel drive, carved my name into his leather seats, …I took a Louisville slugger to both headlights, slashed a hole in all four tires. Maybe next time he'll think before he cheats." I'm guessing he will.

Kill Bill contained so much revenge that it took two movies to complete. It started with *Kill Bill Volume 1* in 2003 and finished with *Kill Bill Volume 2* in 2004. Both movies are the story of Uma Thurman's character going after every individual of a gang that killed her fiancé and family on her wedding day and put her in a coma.

In *A History of Violence* (2005), we are clearly shown that you can never hide your sin for long. It eventually comes to the surface. Tom Stall moved thousands of miles away to escape his past, but in a fluke accident, his face appears on national news and he is discovered. The only way to cover his tracks and protect his new family is to take out everyone who is after him, a move that reveals his true nature to his wife and son.

JUSTICE AND REDEMPTION

Some of the most popular movies include stories of justice. It is when people are bad and they get what they deserve. It is when we stand up and cheer at the end of the movie because good triumphed and evil lost—hopefully in a very painful way. The *Spider-Man* trilogy illustrates this concept of justice very well. No matter how badly Peter Parker is beaten up in his webbed costume, by the end of the film he has defeated his foes.

Who doesn't cheer for Bruce Willis in the *Die Hard* series, Mel Gibson and Danny Glover in the *Lethal Weapon* series, or Sylvester Stallone in the *Rocky* series? God has put within us the desire to see good triumph over evil and watch the weak rise up against the strong.

We also find spiritual parallels in movies about redemption, such as Steven Spielberg's 1993 production of *Schindler's List*, which gives us a fact-based, moving experience of redemption. Oskar Schindler is a vain, glorious, and greedy German businessman who becomes an unlikely humanitarian amid the barbaric Nazi reign when he feels compelled to turn his factory into a refuge for Jews. He literally redeems (purchases) more than 1,100 Polish Jews from the death chambers.

On TV, *Samantha Who?* features lead actor Christina Applegate as Samantha, a materialistic, shallow, philandering liar who gets in a car accident, develops amnesia, and then slowly realizes the error of her old ways. In an *Entertainment Weekly* interview, Applegate says, "We set up this duality of her good and evil. People really relate to righting wrongs in life."[9]

Yes, they do. It is called redemption. Even though Samantha isn't looking to give her life to Jesus to right the wrongs of her past, we can start with where she is. This, by the way, is where people in your community are—aware of their bad choices and relational mistakes and trying so hard in their own power to do better. Yes, they are looking in the wrong place for the answer. But we can celebrate the seeking and help them find their way to the open arms of a God who says, "You matter."

WRAPPING IT ALL UP

Søren Kierkegaard tells us that "if we are to really hear the Gospel, it will be because we overhear it spoken to someone else and realize indirectly that what is being said powerfully relates to us and what is going on in our own lives."[10] That is what we do when we discover God's truth in culture and leverage the opportunity to have a conversation with others. Sometimes this conversation will happen on a personal level, and sometimes it will happen in a public setting, such as a church service.

The first step is tuning in to God's truth in culture, wherever it appears. The next step is figuring out how to use that knowledge to have an impact on our community. To do that, let's consider the dream of a 12-year-old boy...

chapter 7

SCRATCH PEOPLE
WHERE THEY ITCH

Ever since he was a little boy, Thomas Giovante* had an interest in the Democratic Republic of Congo in central Africa. When he was about twelve years old, he read a story in National Geographic about the children of Congo, and it stayed with him for years. He talked to his parents and friends about it and said, "Someday, I'm going to Congo to help!" They loved his passion and encouraged him to pursue his dreams.

However, by the time Thomas graduated from high school, he was focused on sports, medicine, friends, and fun and he mostly forgot about the story that marked him so clearly as a child. He started into college and began pursuing a degree in physical therapy with a minor in business, but he felt empty inside—as if nothing he was doing was worth anything. He watched his parents in the rat race of life making money, spending money, making more money, spending more money— and never having enough. He didn't want that. No, he knew there had to be something more.

By the time he was a junior at the university, Thomas began to attend a weekly Christian gathering on campus. He was not even sure why he went the first time, except he had a gnawing void inside that didn't seem to go away regardless of how many girls he met or frat parties he attended. A friend had kept nagging him to go, so one day when he was wallowing in a depressed state of despair, he finally gave in. To his surprise, he somewhat liked it. Parts of it were weird, and there were some geeks there with whom he for sure did not want to be seen, but there were also some cool people he knew—and a great talk about some of the stuff that was going on inside of him that he had never told anyone.

Through the rest of his junior year, this gathering became a regular part of Thomas' week. He was feeling a new sense of hope and direction for his life. God was doing something deep in his heart, and although he didn't fully understand it, he knew it was marking him for the rest of his life.

At one of the gatherings just before the semester ended, a woman spoke on the plight of the children in the world who were facing poverty and malnutrition. In

---

* Don't try to figure out if you know Thomas Giovante. He is a fictional character but represents several true-life stories I've heard over the years.

a nanosecond, all the memories from the National Geographic story he had read as a child about the Republic of Congo came rushing back into Thomas' mind like a huge ocean wave. As though he had just read the story for the first time, he instantly experienced again all the feelings he had for the people of Congo and the desire to go there and help! Except this time, his dream was infused with a desire to help them spiritually!

Within two months, he dropped out of school, enrolled in a summer training program for short-term missionaries and began raising support to begin his term in Congo that fall. His friends and family quickly noticed his passion and desire to help the people of Congo, so it didn't take long at all to raise the support he needed. By September, he was standing in a village about

God was doing something deep in his heart, and although he didn't fully understand it, he knew it was marking him for the rest of his life.

111

two hundred kilometers north of Kinshasa, at the western edge of the Republic of Congo. His childhood dream was finally coming true.

Through the training he had received over the summer, his passion was stronger than ever to let the people of Congo know how much they matter to God. He wanted them to experience the life-changing grace of Christ that had changed him just a short time ago. He knew that so many of them were dying each day; there wasn't much time to deliver the good news of eternal life!

So he quickly established himself, found a place to live, and started preparing for his first public services. The people of the village watched with curiosity—a strange man living in their village, eating their food, setting up a tent. It was all very strange, but they watched with huge anticipation. Maybe this was the answer. Maybe he was here to offer them the help for which they longed. They had heard of white men in other villages bringing medicine and food and supplies. But up until now, it had been largely a fantasy for them. And so their children continued to die, and their young men continued to turn to fighting and violence. When people got sick, they rarely recovered.

Thomas found an interpreter who knew both English and the native language, Lingàla, and he began making plans for his first public service when he could tell the village residents about Jesus.

It was interesting to Thomas how other missionaries in surrounding villages weren't preaching the good news at all. They had teamed up with UNICEF and other organizations, and they were busy providing food and medicine. Thomas thought that was a worthy effort but wondered why they had abandoned their first calling to deliver the good news of Jesus Christ.

The week finally came when Thomas held his first public meeting. He could see the smiles on the people's faces all week as he handed out flyers inviting them to the first public service. The anticipation was building. He was even second-guessing whether he had brought over a large enough tent from the states and whether the public address system that was purchased for him would be loud enough for the crowd that was sure to gather.

On the first Sunday morning, hundreds gathered for the opening service, spilling out all sides of the tent. Thomas had found a village musician to play songs as people gathered, and that seemed to raise the excitement level even more. When the time came, Thomas stood up to deliver his very first message to the people of this small village in Congo, and it was a great message. A little rough through a translator, but he still felt it was one of his best deliveries ever. He laid out the Gospel presentation in the clearest way he possibly could. He was certain some people would respond.

Massive disappointment.

That is the only way to describe how Thomas felt following that service and in the weeks to come. The crowd that started as several hundred dwindled quickly to less than twenty. The smiles and anticipation that seemed to be all around during his first few weeks in the village turned back to hollow faces filled with desperation. The wailing of adults and children alike every time another villager succumbed to hunger or disease seemed to get louder in Thomas' ears every day.

The dream of Thomas Giovante seemed to die a little more every day. No matter how much he tried or how loud he talked, he couldn't seem to bridge the gap between the hearts of the people and the eternal life that was waiting for them in heaven. If they only understood, if they only would listen, it would change their perspectives and mark their destinies. But they didn't understand, and they wouldn't listen. And so the dream of Thomas Giovante to make a difference in Congo remained a dream.

Within six months, he packed up and headed back home, his head hanging in frustration and shame.

Thomas Giovante had failed. His heart was in the right place. He had great intentions. His motives were pure. But he failed to accomplish his goal of reaching the people of Congo with the Gospel of Christ.

Why did he fail? Why did he not get the results he wanted so badly? What was he doing wrong? You might say he gave up too soon, that if he had just kept at it, eventually he would have started to see some results.

Maybe, but I don't think so. I believe the reason Thomas failed is that he broke a classic missionary rule: *In order to earn the right to be heard, you must meet the needs of the people.*

Thomas did what church planters have been doing in America for decades. He did what many pastors have been trained to do. He did what thousands of frustrated pastors do every Sunday morning. He just stood up and preached *the good news* of a God who loves the whole world, but his listeners didn't feel that love. With great intellect and theological accuracy, he talked of an eternal life with Jesus in heaven but didn't give them an experience of who Jesus is and why they would want to be with him forever. He told them God is love and cares for every one of them, but they didn't feel loved or cared for. He told them stories *about* Jesus but didn't introduce them *to* Jesus.

The people of the village came to the tent after listening to the

Joe,

I've been in churches where I felt preached at, where an angry, saliva-splattering preacher made me think God is angry with me. I've been in revival meetings where some guy came into town and told me about the holiness of God but left before giving me a picture of his love for me. maybe you've experienced that as well. That's a bummer.

It bothers me when church people mess up. well, actually, it bothers me when anyone messes up. I just don't expect it. As a customer service representative, you have probably had similar experiences at your company. Does it ever frustrate you when you hear a story of how another employee has treated a customer? Does it ever make you angry because you know someone isn't representing the company accurately? Do they get all the facts correct but communicate so badly that it turns away the customers?

Anywhere humans are involved in the process, stuff happens. when it happens in a church, it makes me angry, and sometimes embarrassed. In your case, you lose a loyal customer. In our case, we may lose the chance to let someone know how much he or she matters to God. That's a real bummer.

-Tim

cries of their hungry children all night long. On their way to his service, they walked past the hut filled wall-to-wall with mats of dying AIDS patients—most of whom they knew and loved. They walked to the tent with the recent memory of a child who died of diarrhea and the reports of their adolescent sons dying on the front lines of the bloody revolution. Those were the people, the issues, and the problems on their minds. And so when Thomas Giovante talked of a Jesus who cared, they didn't feel it. When he talked of a God who so loved the world, they had never experienced that love. In fact, truthfully, the more Thomas talked, the angrier they became. What type of God would allow the devastation surrounding them? Once again, their hopes were dashed. Starvation and sadness were the only roads ahead for them.

Some of you are angry right now. You are wondering why I told this story in a book about pop culture. No missionary would do this in today's enlightened world. It is beyond comprehension. Maybe thirty or forty years ago, but today's missionary-sending agencies understand the basics of learning the culture and the language and helping meet the basic needs of the community. That may be mostly true in foreign lands, but here is the deal: *Many pastors, born in America and leading churches in America, don't realize they must operate as a missionary in a foreign land.*

That's right. They launched into leading a church without learning the culture or the language. And they are so clueless about the needs in their community that it is as if they are trying to talk a guy into investing in a retirement plan when he just needs money to turn the heat back on so he can keep his family warm through the winter.

LET'S PLAY A GAME

Do a little exercise with me. This won't take long. Just play along. When I say, "go," hold both your hands about one inch in front of your eyes, not much further out than the end of your nose (okay, for some of you that might be two inches). Keep your eyes open and hold your hands there for about five seconds. Ready? Okay, go.

Waiting.

Okay, are you back? What did you see? Not much, right? Your hands were covering most of your view. Perhaps you could see a little peripherally or perhaps between your hands or through your fingers, but for the most part, your vision was blocked.

For someone who is lacking for food or basic medical attention for someone they love, those problems are just like your hands in front of your eyes. It is all they can see. It doesn't matter how eloquent you are or how convincing you can be that God cares, they can't see it. All they can see are the problems right in front of their eyes, and the more you talk about how God cares about their problems, the more clueless they think you are.

Until you help them with the problem, most will not hear you. Until you begin to offer assistance to the sick in the village, food for the children, and education for those who are able to support their families—until you begin to address the problems in front of their eyes, you won't earn the right to be heard.

But when you set up the clinics, bring in the food, and start offering vocational training, you earn the right to be heard. They are willing to hear that God loves them because they see you meeting their needs. They feel the hand of a Savior who cares, and they want to know more. You have helped to move their hands a little further from their faces and the further those hands move, the more they can see clearly the smiling face of Jesus in you.

BUT THIS ISN'T A BOOK ABOUT MISSIONS

Well, it kind of is, but not about reaching people in an impoverished country. It is a book about reaching the community around you, right where you are. However, to do that, you must think like a missionary.

Here is the truth: The people in your community who don't know Christ have a handful of problems right in front of their eyes, and for them, those problems seem as huge, overwhelming, and serious as if they were living in the Republic of Congo. If we want to help them meet Christ, we first have to figure out what the problems are in front of them. Then we can use the people of God and the Word of God to help meet those needs.

In his book, *Pop Goes Religion,** Terry Mattingly says that pop culture can help us identify needs and connect with our community. He writes, "Movies are the books of a culture raised on television. If missionaries came to America, they would immediately recognize this. They would study the moral and religious messages in visual media, seeking insights into the lives of ordinary Americans."

> **I'm not talking about watering down the Gospel.**

117

Mattingly says if you study the popular culture, you can gain insight into the needs of the community. He continues, "This is how missionaries think. But this is not how the vast majority of religious leaders think. As a result, few clergy are taught to think like missionaries. Thus, few believers in the pews know how to make sense out of the images and emotions that help define their lives."[1]

Here is the bottom line: People have needs (Translated: They itch). If you can help meet those needs (Translated: Scratch the itch), you will gain an audience who will be open to the rest of the truth of scripture.

THIS IS NOT JESUS LITE

Let me explain. I'm not talking about watering down the Gospel.

* I have been asked if I knew there was already a book called *Pop Goes Religion*. Absolutely, and it is a great book! Terry is a columnist who often writes about faith and culture, and his book is a compilation of several years of his writings. His book analyzes the faith of people already in the culture, whereas *Pop Goes the Church* considers leveraging the culture to reach people through the local church.

Here is what I know. If you want to reach the unconvinced—those who have not made a commitment to follow Christ—then you need to get their attention. When people don't know God and they aren't convinced that their lives are all that bad without God, the only way to attract them is to offer them something they need. You get their attention by identifying an itch they have and scratching it. That's not necessarily how you *keep* them—but it is often how you *get* them.

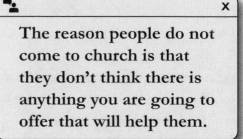

The reason people do not come to church is that they don't think there is anything you are going to offer that will help them.

Thomas would not have had a problem attracting and keeping a crowd if he had been offering food or medical assistance. They would have come by the hundreds and perhaps even thousands. In the meantime, he would have gained respect, developed relationships, and really shown people the love of Jesus.

We do the same thing when we offer help for the needs in our communities. Remember, those needs are many times just as big for them as food and medicine for the people in Congo.

The reason people do not come to church is that they don't think there is anything you are going to offer that will help them. Help them with what? What do they need?

They need help. They have real problems and real issues.

There is a man on his second marriage, it is falling apart just like the first one, and if he cannot figure out how to make this one work, he thinks he'll go crazy. A single mom desperately needs help. Her little kids totally run her life, and it is non-stop stress from morning until night for her. She yells at them all the time and is sure they would be better off without her.

There is an older woman who has chronic pain, and she would

honestly rather be dead. She has been lonely since her husband died, her kids are too busy to care, and she has begun to rely too much on the pain pills the doctor prescribed. A sixteen-year-old boy has been sexually molested by his uncle for two years now. He figures it is his own fault and that something must be wrong with him, and he has begun to experiment with other guys.

There is a middle-aged couple with two teenage daughters. They found out one just became pregnant and they suspect the other one is experimenting with drugs and alcohol. They thought they were good parents, but now they aren't sure. They are mortified that their friends might find out, and the distance and tension between their daughters and them continues to grow.

A young couple with small children has been funding their lifestyle with credit cards for years now. He just lost his job and she is putting in extra hours to try to make up. However, the interest payments alone are killing them. It is stressing their marriage, and they are taking their anger out on their kids. They are just about to lose the house and both cars, and they have no idea where they will go if that happens.

A woman has been yelled at, beaten up, and sexually abused her entire life. Men only want her for one thing. Once they get it, they discard her like an old newspaper. She accepted a new job working for a Christian, which she was so excited about, but now even that guy is starting to hit on her. Her hatred for God is growing exponentially by the day.

That's right. There are men and women and teenagers and children and the elderly in your community that have problems right in front of their eyes—problems that are so big they can't see anything else. They have screwed up or been hurt by others. They have gone through a huge crisis such as the loss of a child or lifelong mate. They are plodding through life with little or no purpose. They are dealing with the consequences of their own regretful choices or the damaging mistakes of others.

For them, you have to help meet those needs first. And so you scratch them where they itch. You identify people's needs and let

Joe,

I want to make sure you don't think this is all a big manipulation trick. I see how it could come across that we scratch your itch so we can get you in the church and put another notch on our salvation belt. Like when someone coaxes his or her runaway dog back in the house with a snack, and then kicks it and locks it up as soon as it falls for the ploy.

That's not it at all. At the heart of this, we want to help you because you matter. There are certain parts of the Bible that will help you more as you are beginning your faith journey and others that will help later. I hope that this won't sound patronizing, but you would never think of learning to drive a semi-truck before you learned how to drive a car. It is a sequencing issue.

In your case, you are well on your way to taking steps. Heck, you've already made it through seven chapters of my book.

-Tim

them know you have some answers they should consider. You are still teaching the Bible. You are just initially choosing to teach the portions of the Bible that address the in-front-of-the-face needs of the people in your community. And you don't just teach truths or quote

Bible verses, but you come along beside them and show them the love of Jesus.

You see, if you don't offer something people need, they won't come. If the people don't come, you can't teach them the truth. So an effective church is busy identifying people's needs and letting the community know you have some help they should consider. If you speak their language, there is a better chance they will come to a service. If they do that, the odds increase significantly that they will hear how much they matter to God, and they just might respond.

If the church of Jesus Christ can offer the world help in dealing with these real needs, we can see the world change! If we can scratch them where they itch, then after they accept Christ and begin to grow in their faith, we can teach principles they don't even know they need yet, such as memorizing scripture, becoming systematic in their giving, and learning how to pray.

Sound like heresy? I will admit I am not a theologian, but I think I have good scriptural backing for this methodology. Read on.

chapter 8

I'M NOT A THEOLOGIAN, BUT...

Right about now, I can hear some of you saying, "Okay, Tim. Slow down. I was tracking with you to a point, but now you are saying we should scratch people where they itch. Have you totally lost your mind? Don't you read the Bible? Are you familiar with Paul's letter to Timothy?"

I have been asked that very question many times. Then, in case I don't have a Bible, the verse is quoted to me:

> Preach the Word; be prepared in season and out of season; correct, rebuke and encourage—with great patience and careful instruction. For the time will come when men will not put up with sound doctrine. Instead, to suit their own desires, they will gather around them a great number of teachers to say what their itching ears want to hear. They will turn their ears away from the truth and turn aside to myths.[1]

A few years ago at Granger, we leveraged the first *Spider-Man* movie to teach about making good choices, sacrificing for what you believe in, and living with purpose. A pastor of a church across town heard about our series and talked about it in his Sunday morning service. He said, "The next several weeks Granger Community Church's messages are going to be about *Spider-Man*. They're going to take the popular culture of a popular movie, and they are going to have that as the theme for their Sunday services, teaching how *Spider-Man* can teach you truths about your spiritual life."

This local pastor continued:

> They're attempting to put the God that they say they serve in a harness with the world popular system. They are putting them together, but according to

what I understand it's not the same God that we serve. I'm sure there are some folks there that know the Lord, but you cannot say you love God and love the world system and yoke them together. If you do the love of the Father is not in you, and I did not say that, the apostle John said that under Holy Spirit inspiration.[2]

This pastor sounds like he's laying out a very valid concern. How can we mix ourselves with the world and still communicate an unpolluted message? Is there any biblical basis for what we are doing? Is he right in saying the love of God is not in you if you choose to leverage the culture to make a difference in your community?

I think those are great questions with which to wrestle. What does the Bible really say?

Before we start, you should know something about me. I'm not a trained theologian. I can't read Greek and I don't know Hebrew. However, I think I am in good company, because it is my guess that the same is true of many of you as well. If so, this chapter might be helpful to you as I provide some bottom shelf principles from the Bible that give a basis for engaging and leveraging the culture through the local church.

If you are a trained theologian, it might help you to know that I had more than fifty seminary-trained men and women help by reviewing this chapter. I am hopeful the next few pages will give you new thoughts about some very old passages of scripture.

These are in no particular order and are by no means exhaustive. Let's start with the book of Acts.

#1—PAUL TALKS TO SOME VIPS
In Acts 17, Paul is in Athens and he is a little bit irritated. He has

been waiting for Silas and Timothy for some time. Without the benefit of text messaging or Facebook, he has no idea if they received the message or when they will be arriving. While he waits, he is checking out the city and finding idols everywhere he looks. It is starting to bother him, and he is wondering what he can do to point the people of Athens toward the loving God that he has personally experienced, instead of these idols made of stone. He has been talking all day to both church people and city people, asking about the idols and telling the story of Jesus and the Resurrection.

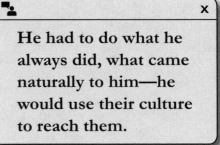

He had to do what he always did, what came naturally to him—he would use their culture to reach them.

But it doesn't seem like he's making much progress. In fact, some of the city folk called him a "babbler." Finally, though, he begins telling the story of Jesus to a person of influence—a person who is intrigued enough to take Paul before the Council of the Areopagus. Now, this is a big deal. This is a group of bigwigs, VIPs, movers and shakers, big shots. When they say "Jump," you ask, "How high?" When someone says, "Show me the money," these are the guys who have it. You get the idea—these were important dudes.

I imagine Paul's mind was swirling with questions: What should he say? How will they receive him? Did they already know that some people in town were saying he was "advocating foreign gods"? Will they be on the defensive? Should he stand at a podium or behind a round table? Should he use Microsoft PowerPoint or Apple's Keynote?

Okay, strike the last two questions. Paul was trying to figure out what to say and how to say it, and he didn't have a whole lot of time to think about it. There is a good chance this meeting took place on a rocky hill that rises 380 feet just below the Acropolis, and Paul probably only had as much time as it took him to walk up the stairway[3] carved into the rock. He didn't have time to come up with a new strategy. He had to do what he always did, what came naturally to him—he would use their culture to reach them.

His first words: "It is plain to see that you Athenians take your religion seriously. When I arrived here the other day, I was fascinated with all the shrines I came across. And then I found one inscribed, 'To the god nobody knows.' I'm here to introduce you to this God so you can worship intelligently, know who you're dealing with."[4]

Whoa. Beginning today, I'm going to rebrand him as Apostle Paul the Genius. Do you see what he did? In his first words to perhaps the most important group to whom he has ever talked, Paul chose to speak their language. He saw they were searching for answers but looking in the wrong places. So he got their attention immediately by talking about something with which they were all familiar—one of their icons, one of the popular images of the day.

He used that image to say, "You are searching. You are longing to know a higher being. Let me tell you about this God you seek." He started with an idol to an unknown god and finished by talking about Jesus. Pure genius.

But that wasn't all.

#2—PAUL QUOTES A SECULAR SONG

It is the same day, same speech. He is still talking to these suits about Jesus, still trying to connect with them. So what does he do next? He quotes lyrics from Sting.

Okay, it wasn't literally Sting, but it was the Sting of his day. He quoted from the Cretan poet Epimenides. He said, "For in him we live and move and have our being." This is word for word from Epimenides. He had it memorized!

Now he's on a roll. He goes on to say, "As some of your own poets have said, 'we are his offspring.'" Here, he is quoting from a poem by Cleanthes called "Hymn to Zeus." Paul is using a song written by a pagan philosopher to a false god to tell people about Jesus!

And who are the philosophers of our day? Musicians and movie producers. To put it in context, Paul is quoting from the Christina Aguilera or Steven Spielberg of his day. Under the inspiration of the Holy Spirit, Paul is quoting the first century version of Dave Mathews, Justin Timberlake, or Eminem, and it is now part of the inspired Word of God.

#3—PAUL USED THE WORDS OF SECULARISTS TO SCOLD CHRISTIANS

When Paul is writing to Titus, he once again quotes from Epimenides. What is interesting this time is that he is using the harsh words of a pagan philosopher, "The Cretans are liars from the womb, barking dogs, lazy bellies,"[5] but he is talking about believers who are causing problems. There are times when it might be appropriate to use words from our secular culture to bring conviction to followers of Christ.

Paul does this another time in his first letter to the Corinthians, where he quotes from the Greek comedy *Thais*, written by the familiar Greek poet Menander. He uses the phrase "Bad company corrupts good character" to encourage the Christians to come to their senses and stop sinning.[6]

But it wasn't only Paul who leveraged the culture.

#4—JESUS PRACTICED REDEEMING THE CULTURE

Did you know Jesus grew up about two miles from the local theater? Nazareth was a small village, and it is likely that Jesus and his dad had to go outside of Nazareth to find work. History tells us that at the time of Jesus, a sophisticated city called Sepphoris* was being built a few miles away with modern streets, a magnificent palace, a gymnasium, mosaic floors, and yes, even a theatre. Not just any theatre—this one likely sat over three thousand people.

It is very possible that Jesus and Joseph even worked on the construction of the theater. The reason historians believe this might be true is Jesus' usage of the word *hypocrite*. This was not a common word. This secular word used in Greek theater referred to an actor who played different roles by wearing different masks. In fact, Jesus was the only person in the Bible to use this word, yet he used it over and over.

Jesus took a common word from the pop culture of his day and he gave it new meaning. He infused it with a moral connotation, as in Matthew 6 when he said we shouldn't parade our giving as the hypocrites who love to be seen, and in Matthew 23 when he used the word seven times to describe the hearts and behavior of the religious leaders. Jesus learned from his pop culture, found purpose in a secular image, and redeemed the culture by giving it new spiritual meaning.

#5—KING LEMUEL WRITES A PROVERB

I have a question for the married men: How many of you read the words of Proverbs 31 to your wife once a week? Every Saturday night, you sit her down and lay it out, "Hey babe, a wife of noble character gets up while it is still dark, and she works vigorously and has strong arms. And you know what else? She buys land, plants a garden, makes clothes to sell on eBay, and her kids think she is cool."

You don't do this? Well, it was typical for a Jewish husband to read

129

* Rob Wegner, pastor of Life Mission at Granger Community Church, is a friend and student of the Bible and pointed me to the history of Sepphoris.

the words from Proverb 31 every Sabbath.[7] Not a bad idea. They are, after all, part of the inspired Word of God. But interestingly, King Lemuel, a secular leader, wrote these words. We don't know much about him, except he wasn't Jewish and he was quite creative.[8]

He was a non-religious dude who wrote creative lyrics. Kind of like the Foo Fighters, or Moby, or the creators of *High School Musical*. (All right, forget the last one, but the other two still count.) Soon every Jewish husband was reading these words to his wife, and every Jewish wife was hoping to be worthy of the words.

Do you get the significance of this? A leader who was not a follower of Christ wrote a poem, and it is now the inspired Word of God! That's right; lyrics from an artist that wouldn't be quoted by many pastors because of their secular nature are now in your Bible.

#6—PARABLES WERE CUTTING EDGE

Did you know that Jesus' usage of parables as a teaching method was not unique to him? He did not create a new method of communicating. Madeleine Boucher, in *Parables*, writes that Jesus "made brilliant use of a genre which was already of long tradition and which was familiar to all throughout the Mediterranean world." She tells of how parables were employed by politicians, philosophers, prophets, and Jewish rabbis and lists specific teachers such as Socrates and Aristotle.[9]

Jesus' usage of parables is "decidedly secular" according to Leland Ryken who said, "On the basis of their literal level, we could not possibly guess that [parables] are designed to teach religious truth. The parables thus assault any 'two-world' outlook that divides the spiritual and earthly realms. In the world of parables, it is in everyday experience that people make their spiritual decisions and that God's grace works."[10]

Interesting. Jesus paid attention to his culture, watched the most effective communicators of the day, and utilized the best methodology. Do you ever wonder if today he would use Second Life, YouTube, and broadband streaming as methods to deliver truth? I do.

What better example do we have in today's world than the *parables* that can be derived from pop culture? Richard Leonard says specifically about movies, "The cinema's parables can provide us with a venue in which to fulfill the great commission."[11]

#7—TOPICAL TEACHING WAS A SPECIALTY OF JESUS

It is an age-old debate: Should churches teach verse by verse, tackling topics as they come out of the text (this is called "expository" teaching)—or is it acceptable to pick a topic (such as finding purpose, dealing with anger, or raising a child) and then teach on verses throughout the Bible which address that issue?

Some say that teaching topically on a felt need of the congregation is bending to "what their itching ears want to hear."[12] I could not disagree more. Teaching on a topic that meets the needs of your people is not only biblical; it is following the example of Jesus. Rick Warren says, "Jesus frequently asked people, 'What do you want me to do for you?' God uses all kinds of human needs to get people's attention."[13] In addition, Ephesians 4:29 tells us we should speak "only what is helpful for building others up according to their needs, that it may benefit those who listen." Warren concludes, "Notice that what we say should be determined by the needs of the people to whom we are speaking. It only stands to reason that if this is God's will for our conversations, it

> Teaching on a topic that meets the needs of your people is not only biblical; it is following the example of Jesus.

131

must also be God's will for our sermons."

Richard Leonard points out, "The parables do not mention God. They rarely have a religious setting. Jesus takes ordinary events of daily life and draws out lessons about faith, hope, love, justice, fidelity, self-esteem, prudence, mercy, and hospitality."[14] Since Jesus had the books of the Old Testament available to him, it seems he would have taught verse by verse instead of topically if that were his prescribed method, but he rarely did.

We even find a clear example of Jesus being culturally astute and addressing some big news stories that everyone was talking about in Luke 13. He mentioned the Galileans whom Pilate had just killed while they were worshiping, and then talked about the eighteen people who died when the tower in Siloam fell on them.[15]

#8—JESUS DID NOT AVOID THE CULTURE

Jesus said, "My prayer is not that you take them out of the world but that you protect them from the evil one."[16] Tom Wright expands on this and says, "The 'world,' remember, in this Gospel doesn't mean simply the physical universe as we know it. It means the world insofar as it has rebelled against God, has chosen darkness rather than light, and has organized itself to oppose the creator."[17] Jesus is not only leaving us on earth, but he is leaving us in a flawed worldly system so that we might have an impact.

It was clear that Jesus did not avoid the common places where people in the culture hung out, even though there were questionable activities happening there. He went to parties, drank wine, and was seen with the most dishonest and deceptive people in the community.[18] He broke several religious rules by being alone, in conversation, with a very immoral woman, and even drinking from her cup.[19] And he allowed a prostitute to show him affection, in public, to the dismay of a religious leader.[20]

Joe,

Does this jack with your view of Jesus? When you read that he "went to parties, drank wine, and was seen with the most dishonest and deceptive people in the community," what does that make you think? Do you cheer because you think Jesus was a partier? Or do you get sad and question his integrity?

The Bible is clear, Jesus never sinned. I think what we learn from him is that it is possible to hang out with normal, everyday people without compromising your own integrity. I'm not saying you have no integrity or that a Christian is perfect. I'm just saying that sometimes Christians have made the mistake of totally withdrawing from all their relationships outside the church, and it has been hurtful. maybe you've lost a friend to the church this way. maybe it is one of the reasons you keep the church at arm's length.

-Tim

133

#9—PAUL THE CHAMELEON?

Some have accused Paul, based on his words, of being a chameleon.

> To the Jews I became like a Jew, to win the Jews.
> To those under the law I became like one under the
> law…so as to win those under the law. To those
> not having the law I became like one not having the
> law…so as to win those not having the law. To the

weak I became weak, to win the weak. I have become all things to all men so that by all possible means I might save some.[21]

It sounds as if the end justifies the means. As long as someone accepts Christ, whatever method you used is suddenly sanctified, right? I don't think so, but I do love Paul's heart. If I can take the liberty to put this in my own words, I think he might have been saying, "I'm not going to violate any essentials of the faith or non-negotiable beliefs—but I'll ditch my preferences and methodologies in a second if it means I might help introduce someone to Christ."

#10—YOUR EVERYDAY LIFE

Paul writes to the Gentiles in Rome:

> Take your everyday, ordinary life—your sleeping, eating, going-to-work, and walking-around life—and place it before God as an offering…Don't become so well-adjusted to your culture that you fit into it without even thinking. Instead, fix your attention on God. You'll be changed from the inside out. Readily recognize what he wants from you, and quickly respond to it. Unlike the culture around you, always dragging you down to its level of immaturity, God brings the best out of you, develops well-formed maturity in you.[22]

Eugene Peterson summarized that passage quite nicely. I wonder if, thinking through the lens of leveraging culture, this passage could also be paraphrased in this way:

Take your everyday, ordinary life—going to the
movies, watching TV, listening to your XM radio,
flipping through the pages of *People Magazine*—and
place it before God as an offering. Don't become so
well-adjusted to your culture that you fit into it without even thinking. Instead, always be looking for God
in the culture. You'll be changed from the inside out.
While sitting on the couch surfing channels or listening to the Top 20 on the radio, always be looking for
what God wants you to do and who he wants you to
be, and quickly respond to it. Don't let the culture
drag you down to its level, but maintain an awareness
of God in the culture and keep watching for the next
step you can take toward Christ.

AND NOW FOR THE BENEDICTION

Congratulations! It might seem amazing to you, but you just
finished a chapter on the theology of leveraging pop culture in the
church. It wasn't exhaustive, but I'm hoping it gave you reason and
desire to study further.

Now we are turning a big corner. We are moving away from
theology and away from theory. This is where it starts to get
very practical.

chapter 9

CREATE A LITTLE BUZZ

There are several different definitions for *buzz*, including a short haircut, a feeling you get while intoxicated, and a low altitude fly-by in an airplane. I'll leave it to other authors to explore those topics. My interest is in the final definition for buzz: "A particularly intense kind of word of mouth." The Merriam-Webster's Online Dictionary defines buzz this way: "To utter covertly by or as if by whispering."

This is referring to the type of buzz that can happen about your business, organization, or church. Buzz is what happens when you have a product or offer a service, and your guests are talking about it to their friends. You aren't paying them to talk about it. You didn't ask them to talk about it. They just are. That's buzz.

Buzz is what happens when fifteen hundred inmates in Cebu, Phillipines practice a routine spoofing *Thriller* by Michael Jackson. A guard uploads a video onto YouTube and soon the world is buzzing. It has now been viewed more than eleven million times.[1]

Buzz is what happens when a reader reviews a book on Amazon.com, which you then read and purchase because of the opinion of a *real* person, or when you pick a hotel, not based on the hotel's website, but based on the buzz about the hotel from user reviews found on TripAdvisor.com.

Buzz is what happens when you blog about your recent experience at the Honda dealership, or you love your Harley so much you create a personal website to connect with other Harley owners, or you participate in an online forum shared by other owners of that new digital camera you just bought.

Buzz is what happens when your lawyers, your communications team, or your head of marketing did not pre-approve the message. Rather, it is what happens when consumers use their own time and resources to create, distribute, and consume information about your brand (i.e. your church or product).

The first time I remember seeing this in large scale was several years ago with the release of the movie *The Blair Witch Project* (1999). This started as a low-budget American horror movie that was never supposed to make it to the big screen. In fact, the producers were just hoping to get it on cable. It cost $22,000 to produce, but they used the

> Buzz: "A particularly intense kind of word of mouth."

power of *word of mouth marketing* on college campuses to perpetrate the myth that the movie was true. Before long, the buzz had a life of its own and by the time it was done, the movie had grossed $241 million worldwide. It still stands in the *Guinness Book of World Records* as having the highest profit-to-cost ratio of a motion picture ever, making back over ten thousand dollars for every dollar spent.[2]

Mark Hughes says in *Buzzmarketing* that we talk about six tried and true things: "the unusual, outrageous, taboo (sex, lies, etc.), hilarious, remarkable, or secretive."[3] He says what gets us buzzing to others are things rooted in emotion, subjects that surprise or thrill us, that which makes us laugh, or things where you gasp and say "You've got to be kidding!"

RECENT EXAMPLES

As I write this, several examples come to mind from recent months that have caused the entire country, sometimes even the world, to buzz:

- In April 2007, a mentally ill Korean student barricaded himself in a classroom building and opened fire on the campus of Virginia Tech. He killed thirty-two students and professors before ending his own life. It was the deadliest school shooting in American history, and the entire world buzzed, unable to fathom the carnage that one lonely depressed individual had inflicted.

139

- After an entire year of very public ups and downs (mostly downs), Britney Spears lost custody of her children in October 2007, after being found guilty of habitual and frequent abuse of controlled substances. In January 2008, television crews filmed her as she was forcibly removed from her home and taken away for psychiatric evaluation. The world buzzed as the downward spiral of this celebrity continued.

- In early 2007, Steve Jobs announced the introduction of a new phone that would forever change the technology of talking to each other. It was called the *iPhone* and was hyped to be God's gift to artistic geeks everywhere. People stood in line for days before the June 30 release of the phone and shelled out more than six hundred dollars for the privilege of being an early adopter. A few months later, the craze continued as Apple released new versions of the *iPod* including the *iPod Touch*. Rumors are that Apple is working on an *iDishwasher*, *iLawnmower* and the long-awaited *iEye* (for those with poor vision).*

WHO CARES?

Emanuel Rosen, in his book *The Anatomy of a Buzz*, says that this concept of buzz is more important for us to understand now than it has ever been. There are three factors in today's society, he says, that make buzz so powerful.[4] First, people cannot hear you. There is so much noise in the world that we are forced to tune out everything just to stay sane. So we tune into what seems viral more than what seems institutional.

Secondly, people don't trust you. Because of all the public failures of corporations, government and churches, most people are skeptical of anything an institution says about itself. If it came from the institution, it must be a lie.

The third factor why buzz is so powerful is because people are

* I admit it…I totally fabricated this sentence.

so connected. They don't need your pastor or leaders to say anything about your church. They can hop online and see what twenty people are saying about your church right now, and it is totally unfiltered (i.e. unblemished by the corporate-ese). That is why buzz is a bigger factor today than it has ever been.

Here is why this matters so much: If you want to reach people in your community, you need to get their attention. Putting an advertisement in the newspaper or sending out a postcard isn't cutting it anymore in most communities. Those might be good secondary tools, but what if you could figure out a way to get the people in your community talking about what your church is doing?

Allow me to share an example…

MYLAMESEXLIFE.COM

It was a normal February in northern Indiana, which means there were about twelve inches of snow on the ground, temperatures below zero, and a lot of talk of hope for an early spring. Not much else was happening until one afternoon when four billboards quietly went up around town.

The billboards contained only one image and no words except a website address. The image was of two pairs of intertwined bare feet hanging out the end of a bed. Although you could only see the feet, it was obvious the couple knew each other quite well. The website link was MyLameSexLife.com.*

That was it. No company name. No indication of who was sponsoring the billboards. Just the picture of the feet and the website address.🖥️⁾

We sponsored these billboards at Granger Community Church as an intentional effort to create buzz in the community based on a conversation already happening. We wanted to do something different.

---

* We kept the website link "live," so check it out.

🖥️⁾ KEYWORD: SEX | PopGoesTheChurch.com

To offer something unique. To create a stir in the community. For weeks before these boards were put up, we told our congregation, "Get ready. You will have an opportunity to have a conversation with a friend, neighbor, or co-worker. Be ready for the conversation. Decide now what you are going to say. Be prepared to invite your friend to 'come and see.'" They were ready, and they did invite.

The MyLameSexLife.com website featured a thirty-second flash video asking some open-ended questions about relationships and love, then led them to our church website where they were invited to join us for the five-week series.

Prior to the launch of the series, we were averaging 5,000 people each weekend. The first weekend after the series launched, attendance jumped by more than 2,000 people to 7,300. During the remainder of the series, our attendance didn't drop below 6,500. In the final analysis, the series gave us an overall increase of 800 people.

Within a couple hours of the billboards going up, the phone started ringing. The buzz had begun. We didn't have to call newspapers or TV stations or put out a press release—they called us. Every local news network ran multiple stories on the billboards. A full-color picture of the billboard was printed on the front page of the local paper with the caption, "What About Those Feet?"[5] Local talk radio programs were taking calls to discuss the rightness or wrongness of the billboards. A reporter attended the first weekend and wrote a lengthy article in the newspaper about her experience. She pretty much outlined every point of the message.

By the first weekend, senior pastor Mark Beeson had been interviewed several times on the *Fox News Channel* and on the Mancow nationally syndicated radio program. Newspapers and television stations all over the country picked up the story. The buzz wasn't just local—it was national. 💻⁾

💻⁾ KEYWORD: SEX | PopGoesTheChurch.com

Joe,

You might have noticed, sometimes the stuff we do in the church is cheesy. In fact, sometimes it is dripping with cheese. I think there is a fine line between creating buzz and being cheesy. This billboard idea created buzz the first time, but if we had done it every month, it would have quickly become a gimmick.

I think someone like you has a much better perspective on cheesiness than we do. I wish more church leaders could get into your mind and see through your eyes. It would be incredibly valuable.

-Tim

But let's step back for a minute and analyze the results. Was this series a success because we got on TV? Uh, nope. Was it a win because our attendance went up by two thousand people? No.

Here is why it was a win: Because a whole bunch of people figured out a church had something to say that actually made a difference in their lives. It was a win because a couple thousand people—some who had already decided they were worthless—heard how much they matter to God. It was a win because six weeks following the series, we saw 833 people make a public decision to follow Christ on a single weekend.🖥

WE'RE NOT JUST TALKING ABOUT SEX

You might be thinking that buzz with a sex series is a no-brainer.

🖥 KEYWORD: 833 | PopGoesTheChurch.com

Everyone knows sex sells. My example was about a sex series, but positive buzz about your church can also come as a result of unexpected care. Buzz can come when you make a follow-up phone call to someone just to make sure she received a personal touch. Buzz can happen when you are flexible and actually let someone come in the auditorium with his cup of coffee—or when you offer wireless internet during the services.* Buzz comes, one person at a time, when you offer care and love and help to those who are hurting.

We've made an intentional effort to have a real impact in our inner city in recent years. For more than five years at Granger, we have given away 150,000 pounds or more of food each year to the area agencies and charities. In 2006, in celebration of our twentieth anniversary, we gave a gift to twenty different community efforts during "20 Days of Giving." Rather than celebrate our anniversary by making it all about us, we did things such as providing scholarships for public school students for an educational field trip they couldn't afford, helping the under-served with heating bills, and giving hundreds of blankets to an agency that helps teenage moms. This was certainly buzz-worthy.

In recent years, we have been developing a community center to serve a neighborhood in downtown South Bend where the average annual household income is $7,300. This center will house an alternative high school, after-school tutoring, GED classes, life skills training, a coffee house, a health and wellness referral center, and an arts and vocational training center. It is starting to generate momentum and the buzz is happening. In June 2007, the city of South Bend (yes, the government!) joined our project and gave us $100,000 to continue the renovations. That sure created buzz!

---

* If you haven't picked up a copy of *First Impressions: Creating Wow Experiences in your Church* by Mark Waltz, you should. He outlines practical help for creating memorable experiences for guests at your church.

CAUTIONS ABOUT BUZZ

It is important to note before closing this chapter that creating buzz is not the goal. If you just want to create buzz, go hire a stripper to dance in your lobby. Tell everyone that if you do not meet your goal for the building campaign, you are going to kill yourself. Show up next week at church in only your underwear, or sell WWJD thongs (not the ones for your feet) in your church bookstore.

Merely creating buzz is not the goal. Pushing the envelope or going over the edge is not the point. You aren't trying to get the attention of the community for the sake of attention. Your goal, I presume, is to see people give their lives to Jesus and start walking a new path. You want to help people take steps in their relationships toward Christ. Wherever they are along their spiritual journey, you want to see them take a step or two.

It is incredibly easy to forget the purpose and fall prey to gimmicks. You do a sex series because another church did it and got lots of attention. You add smoke, fog, and lights because it is cool. Your pastor preaches in ripped jeans and an untucked shirt because his favorite mentor does.

The outsider can smell a fake a mile away. In fact, they come in assuming you are fake. If you've employed a bunch of gimmicks and don't deliver any authenticity, they will be out of there before you can cue the haze.

Before you do anything in hopes of creating buzz, check your heart. Make sure your motives are to help people know how much they matter to God. Make sure you are able to deliver an unforgettable experience for your guests so they will actually want to return. Work hard on the message so you have something to say that will help them see Jesus.

So you created a little buzz, people came to check it out... now what?

145

chapter 10

THE BEATLES AND DESPERATE HOUSEWIVES GO TO CHURCH

"Great book so far, Stevens—but make it practical. I want to leverage the culture, but what do I do?"

I am glad you asked. Books filled with theory are a dime a dozen. If you ever write one, don't send it to me, because I probably won't read it. I'm interested in theory, but only if it is connected to something tangible. The *why* is good—but it is not enough. I need to hear the *how*. I need to see where it is working and what has been tried. I guess there is a little bit of "doubting Thomas" in me. I mentally can agree with something, but it is so helpful to touch it, feel it, and hear from someone who has experienced it.

Joe,

It is very curious to me that you are still reading the book. I'd love it if you would send me a note and tell me why. Don't get me wrong; I'm glad you are. It has been my dream to write this book in a way that would challenge church leaders, while at the same time pique the curiosity of the unchurched. It must be working, but I'm not sure why.

This chapter really gets into some practical ways the church can be less abrasive, and hopefully even attractive, to you. Like I said before, please don't view the ideas here as manipulative tactics to suck you into a vortex of religious extremism. It's not that at all. We just know many churches have been doing it ineffectively for a long time, so we want to do better. That's our hope.

Seriously, hop on to PopGoesTheChurch.com and leave a comment. I'd love to hear from you.

-Tim

So the rest of this book is devoted to the *how*. Since you have read this far, you understand the thesis—the church must leverage the culture if we are going to impact our communities and help people realize how much they matter to God. So now, it is time to pop the hood and let you see exactly how it works. In the next few chapters, I'm going to throw a bunch of ideas at you—some of which we have tried at Granger and others from churches across America.

For this chapter, we will begin by looking at five very specific and practical ways you can leverage the popular culture in your church services.

USE POP CULTURE TO RAISE QUESTIONS

We've already established that there is nothing wrong with the music and art that come out of the Christian culture. However, an overwhelming percentage of it is dogmatic. It strongly states the truth about God. That works well for Christians, because we tend to agree about the truth being proclaimed, so it makes us feel good when we can join with other followers of Christ to experience the artistic communication of that truth.

When we sing old hymns such as "How Great Thou Art" or "Holy, Holy, Holy," we are singing truths about God. Even newer music such as "Awesome is the Lord Most High" by Chris Tomlin or "Revolutionary Love" by David Crowder is written to proclaim truth *about* God or our love *to* God.

However, sometimes in the flow of a church service, you would like to take people from here to there, from point A to point B. Sometimes you are aware there are people attending who are not ready to proclaim their love to God yet. They are tired and worn out and a little bit beaten up, and they need to be convinced.

You can use pop culture to help lift their eyes toward God. You take them where they are, and through the creative and strategic programming of a service, you hold their hands and walk them a little closer to Jesus.

During the month of December 2007, we offered a series of services at Granger called "Let it Be Christmas," and we used the music of the Beatles each week to ask a question. Some church leaders wondered, "Why would you use the music of the Beatles? Don't you know they were totally immoral and anti-Christian?" We didn't use Beatles music because we believed it pointed people to Jesus. We used it so we could connect with our community, consider some questions, and use the Bible to point people to Jesus.

The Beatles' music gave a voice to a generation. They sang about human longing for love, change, justice, and revolution. And this Jesus we serve has answers to the longings about which the Beatles sang. So we used the music of the Beatles to ask a question and the Bible as a source to find the answer.

In one service, "Eleanor Rigby," a sad song about all the lonely people in the world, was performed. We followed with a message about the amazing love of God and the relationship he wants with each of us. The next week, the familiar Beatles' words, "You say you want a revolution" were sung, connecting with virtually everyone in the room who could identify with this desire to change our broken world. The service ended with a message which acknowledged that this world is broken but which described the revolutionary love that Jesus offers.

The music of the Beatles enabled us to pull people in who wouldn't otherwise be listening. We were able to answer questions using the Bible because we got their attention by letting the Beatles ask the question.

I realize this is heresy to some pastors. They would never consider using a secular song[1] in their church services. Even now you are wondering how I can encourage churches to pull music from the world into a worship service. How can I suggest that a song not written to point anyone toward God could be used to accomplish God's purposes on Sunday morning?

It all has to do with how you view your services. Your service probably contains several elements, including announcements, congregational singing, performance music, perhaps drama, and a message. You can view these as separate elements that stand alone in accomplishing a purpose, or you can view your service as one seamless experience that builds toward a goal. If you see it as a seamless experience, then you might use a secular element to open people's hearts to receive a truth that comes later in the service. You might use a secular drama featuring a married couple fighting about money to prompt people to think about their own lives and prepare them to hear a message about God's plan for financial peace.

Or you might use a popular secular song to open people's hearts about their past, so when the pastor talks about what to do with personal shame, they are ready to hear God's Word. They may already be thinking, "That's me. I've messed up. How could this have happened to me?"

The next week, when they hear that song on the radio, they may be instantly pulled back to the service. They may remember again that God has a plan for them, that he can help them start over. Maybe they will remember a decision they made in that service.

Not every element in your service has to be prescriptive. Yes, you are trying to teach a principle or encourage people to consider a truth, but you can use certain elements to raise questions and other elements to help provide answers. A song can get people thinking about the pain in their relationships, the longing in their souls, or the beauty of a flower—and can be the perfect vehicle to prepare your congregation to hear the message.

I have talked to pastors who have never allowed a secular song in their services. I've asked, "Have you ever quoted a secular author, or poet, or historical figure?" The answer is always, "Yes." Perhaps they quoted from an article in *Time* magazine, from a line in a Shakespeare play, or from an episode of *The Oprah Winfrey Show*. Why do they do that? To make a point. They do it to get people thinking, to illustrate a contrast, or to open people's hearts. I then challenge them to stretch that philosophy to cover the entire service. Look at the entire service as one seamless message comprising different elements, all of which are focused on helping people take their next step toward Christ.

Paul did this when he quoted from a famous poet of the day.[2] He wasn't saying, "I agree with everything this poet wrote." He wasn't saying, "Read all his poems." He was just using a well-known poem to connect with his listeners in order to effect change in their lives.[*]

REMEMBER THE THREE-LEGGED STOOL

Three crucial components for planning effective church services have the potential of impacting lives. When I look back at services we planned at Granger that were amazing, it is because all three of the components were strong. When I look back at services that were weak or ineffective, it is because we didn't pay attention to one or more of these components:

Relevant Topic

Cultural Theme   Biblical Truth

Think of these components as a three-legged stool. Without one, the stool falls over. You can have two strong legs, but if the third leg is shorter or weaker than the others are, the potential of a structural failure is probable.

* Another passage to consider is 1 Corinthians 14:22-25. Although it is regarding the use of tongues in the church, the underlying principle is that visitors should understand our public services.

Building a series around a **Relevant Topic** is crucial. The people in your community have real problems and need real help. If you can offer a series of talks on parenting, marriage, managing money, making a difference in the world, addictions, anger, loneliness, purpose, or scores of additional relevant topics, you have the opportunity to connect with your community. Without a relevant topic, people will not listen. They will feel like you are talking *at* them and not *to* them.

A **Cultural Theme** gets them there. When you tackle the topics already portrayed in the culture, such as justice and redemption, it makes it compelling for someone to come for the first time. When you use a pop culture medium to raise issues such as love and sex, or life after death, it makes it easy for someone to invite a friend to come with him or her. Building our recent Christmas series around the music of the Beatles compelled hundreds of people to come who don't normally attend church. Offering a series of services on how to live a life of integrity in your job worked well for us in the fall of 2007, but we would not have had the crowd we did without calling it *The Office* and pulling in illustrations from that popular TV show. You can leverage pop culture as an easy invite for people who don't normally attend[*]

> Without a relevant topic, people will not listen. They will feel like you are talking *at* them and not *to* them.

A church service without a **Biblical Truth** is just a show. Nothing wrong with a show, but that is not what the church is in the *business* of providing. We aren't offering self-help clinics. We don't want just to make people feel good or give them a warm fuzzy experience. We want that experience to include the grace and love of Jesus. We want them to align their lives with the Bible because we know the peace,

153

---

[*] See the chapter on *Stuff* for several more examples from Granger Community Church.

strength, and freedom they will gain when they do that.[3]

USE POP CULTURE TO GET PEOPLE LAUGHING

Most people walk into church for the first time reluctantly. They don't trust the pastor even though they have never met him or her. They assume the people will be weird. They wonder if their children will be well cared for, and they have low expectations for the quality and content of the service.

They walk in and sit down with an Alcatraz-like defense built around them. Their arms are crossed and their ears are closed. It is going to be hard for them to hear how much they matter to God because they don't yet trust the person saying it.

Occasionally, it is good just to do something funny. It might have nothing to do with your topic, but it has everything to do with your effectiveness because it gets people laughing. Laughing is one of the best ways to lower the defenses of your crowd, to get them to move from leaning back with arms crossed to leaning forward with anticipation.*

You can use pop culture to get people laughing. Perhaps it is a movie clip of Jim Carrey discovering his gifts in *Bruce Almighty* (2003) or Will Ferrell saying the prayer to baby Jesus in *Talladega Nights: The Ballad of Ricky Bobby* (2006). Maybe you use a drama to make fun humorously of how the world sometimes views Christians.

USE POP CULTURE TO TEACH BIBLE STORIES

In today's culture, I find many people do not know the stories of the Bible. Since more than half the people who attend church at Granger were previously *unchurched*, there are many Bible stories they

* Log on to GCCWired.com and check out the Media Player for examples of humor used in services at Granger.

KEYWORD: FUNNY | PopGoesTheChurch.com

have never heard. Even among those who grew up going to church, many of them either weren't tuned in or weren't taught about many of the great stories. So when the preacher says "It is just like when Nathan pointed his finger at David," the minds of a bunch of people begin to wander because they have never heard the story.

You can use pop culture to help you teach Bible stories so they will stick, so they will be remembered. One time we took a popular *Saturday Night Live* sketch called "The Culp Family Musical Performances"* and re-enacted it to teach the story of Joseph. The Culps were two recurring characters on *SNL* featuring Marty Culp, an awkward, balding, middle-aged man, and his wife Bobbi Mohan-Culp, who teaches alongside her husband at Altadena Middle School. They perform at various school functions, singing medleys of recent pop songs in their ultra-conservative style. Marty plays the keyboard and sings backup, while Bobbi leads the singing with her high-pitched, operatic vocals.🖥⁾

Dan and Lisa Vukmirovich† rewrote and performed at Granger a six-minute sketch with the Culps teaching the story of Joseph. Using pop songs, awkward transitions, and geeky antics, they told the story of Joseph, including the time he had a dream as a boy, being sold by his brothers, rising to power in Potiphar's house, being thrown into prison, rising to power again in Egypt, and ending with his reencounter with his father and brothers. It was brilliant, hilarious, and effective. One person wrote us and said, "I learned more about the life of Joseph from the Culps than I knew from twenty years growing up in church."

155

---

* The Culps were featured on Saturday Night Live over twenty times between 1996 and 2002.

🖥⁾ KEYWORD: CULPS | PopGoesTheChurch.com

† Dan is an amazingly gifted pastor of music and drama at Granger. His skills are only overshadowed by the talents of his wife Lisa who is a singer, actor, and scriptwriter.

Another time, Mark Beeson (lead pastor at Granger) had a passion and desire to teach the church principles from the life of David, from his days as a shepherd boy, to his friendship with Jonathan, to his legacy as King. We wondered how we were going to make a series on the life of a guy who lived thousands of years ago interesting and

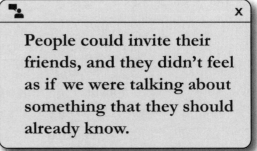

People could invite their friends, and they didn't feel as if we were talking about something that they should already know.

relevant for today's culture. What would motivate an *unchurched* person to come to that series?

So we began asking, "What are the relevant issues from David's life that are true in today's culture?" He was always in the spotlight. He was high profile. When he messed up or did well, everyone knew. So we called the series simply "Dave" and used a paparazzi theme. The promotion image was the cover of a magazine with article headlines (which tied directly to the messages each week) as follows:

- The 5-Stone Challenge: The workout that will take down the *giants* in your life.
- Secret Obsession: What happens when you try to hide it?
- The Private Life of a Warrior: The inside scoop from Dave's best friend Jonathan.🖳⁾

The series rocked. We were able to teach a Bible story from the Old Testament and make it current. People could invite their friends, and they didn't feel as if we were talking about something that they should already know.

🖳⁾ KEYWORD: DAVE | PopGoesTheChurch.com

156

LOOK FOR WAYS TO REDEEM THE CULTURE

There are times when you can leverage culture to reach people, while at the same time reinterpreting it for the culture. Like Jesus did with the word *hypocrite* as we discussed in a previous chapter, you can take popular images or concepts from today's culture and infuse them with new meaning.

We did this a few years ago with *Desperate Housewives*, the hot new show which premiered on ABC in the fall of 2004. If you saw the commercials, it looked like a show filled with deceit, immorality, lying, murder, revenge, and, to some degree, it contained all that stuff. But in the first couple of seasons, it was the highest rated primetime show on TV.* So we asked, "Why?" What is it that is capturing the heart of our culture? What are the themes in this show to which people are connecting?

This was a show about five women and their failures and successes as wives and mothers. So we launched a series on Easter and devoted it to the topic of marriage and parenting. We wanted to help *reinterpret* this new popular show for people. We wanted to help people think about the longings of their hearts, the God-given desires we all have that become messed up because of our baggage and the bad advice of our culture.

One week, we showed a video clip from the show where Lynette is upset that Bree spanked her children without permission. She pours her heart out to her husband, Tom, saying, "My mom beat me and I'm not going to do that to my kids." Tom says that time-outs and threats are not working anymore—they have to figure out something else. Showing this clip immediately helped the parents in our crowd identify with the same struggles that they have disciplining

157

* It is still popular. The first episode of *Desperate Housewives* (ABC) in 2008 (halfway through its fourth season) was the highest-rated non-sports show of the week with more than twenty million viewers.

their kids.🖥⁾

Another week, we showed a clip of Gabrielle talking with her priest about her sins. She wanted a quick blessing to forgive her so she could go on sinning. She ended with disappointment saying that she was sure she could not be forgiven for all the things she had done, and who in our churches does not have a past about which they are embarrassed? This video clip enabled people to identify quickly with feelings of unworthiness before a holy God.

A FINAL THOUGHT

Singing the music of the Beatles, using video clips from *Desperate Housewives*, and acting out a sketch from *Saturday Night Live* may seem like strange ways to help people meet Jesus. But remember, we are cross-cultural missionaries, and as effective missionaries, we must learn the culture of the people we are trying to reach and communicate the Gospel in the language, signs, symbols, and very soil of that culture.

It is probably a good time to repeat the verse I started with at the beginning of this book. The Gospel of John says Christ "became flesh and blood and moved into the neighborhood."[4] Jesus immersed himself in his culture. He used the language, adopted the teaching style, and illustrated his stories using the symbols and icons of the day. He did it to communicate the Gospel of an upside down kingdom.

It is our job to do no less.

Do you want some tips on how to get started? Flip the page.

🖥⁾ KEYWORD: DESPERATE | PopGoesTheChurch.com

chapter 11

LET'S GET IT STARTED

Any good psychiatrist considers his first session with you an assessment. He wants to know the symptoms of your problem and needs enough time to peel back a few layers to gain some insight into your world. Until he knows where you are, he can't decide whether to meet again, send you to someone else, or give you a prescription.

The same is true of a physical therapist. He can't figure out how to help you regain motion in your injured arm until he knows how badly you have been injured. An orthodontist can't put a set of braces in your mouth until she takes some X-rays and makes some molds.

> **Bad change will cause people to leave your church. Good change will also cause people to leave your church.**

And I can't tell you the next step your church should take without knowing where you have been, where you are, and where you would like to go. I do know every church has a next step. Every church could be doing something else to make a bigger difference in its community, but you will have to make that assessment. Knowing your next step is dependent on knowing where you are.

You might be asking, "How do you expect me to do this in my small-town, traditional church with a ninety-year old organist and one part-time pastor?" While someone else says, "I'm the music pastor in a large church, but I don't have the influence to change the direction. What am I supposed to do?"

Many readers are not employed at all by a church. You might be saying, "I'm a volunteer and would love to see my church be better at reaching my friends, but I don't know how." Still others are saying, "I stopped going to church because I couldn't find one that wasn't boring. How do I find a church like the one you are talking about?"

Then there are detail people out there who want to know, "Won't we get sued if we use a movie clip in our service?"

I cannot answer every question, but here's a stab at a few common topics.

START SLOWLY

Change is hard. Change requires time. Changing too slowly frustrates leaders, and changing too quickly intensifies emotions. Bad change will cause people to leave your church. Good change will also cause people to leave your church.

If your church is very traditional and it has never engaged the culture in the ways I described, then you will want to start very slowly. You might begin by using illustrations in the messages from pop culture. Start by using some *safe* clips from shows that are older or family friendly.

Later, you might want to plan and offer one culturally engaging series. Begin talking to your congregation about it for months in advance. Let them know you are going to do a four-week series that is specifically for their friends and neighbors who don't go to church. Talk about some of the things you are going to do in the series (illustrations, promotions, music) that will help build a bridge to introduce their friend to Jesus. Don't scare them. Don't tell them you will be doing this every week from now on. Just let them know it is one four-week series.

Then watch for the results. If you do that series well, new people will begin attending your church and some of them will make a decision to follow Christ. You will probably experience a sharp spike in attendance during the series. People might ask, "Why don't we do this every week?"

But don't do it again—at least not right away. Take time to talk about it with your leaders, to discuss methodology, and perhaps the next year, you can plan two such series.

PROVIDE EXPOSURE

I have seen this work over and over again. Anytime our leadership team has wanted to introduce significant change in the church, we have found a way to expose them to some place it is already happening. When we wanted to construct a building that didn't look like a church, we took a busload of leaders on a tour of buildings in the Midwest. When we wanted to build a children's center that looked more like a McDonalds PlayPlace than a church nursery, we paid all the expenses so nine key leaders could get on a plane and visit interactive children's centers in three different states. When we wanted to convince our congregation to pay for that children's center, we showed them video from the tour.

When we wanted to change our structure and eliminate all our committees, we bought every leader in the church a copy of *The Purpose-Driven Church* and brought them together for video teaching by Rick Warren. When we began to talk about launching additional campuses, we gathered our leaders and brought in an expert who told stories of churches that have seen tremendous results through multi-site ministries.

Telling people about change makes them scared. Showing them gives them vision. Telling them you are thinking about using new elements in your service—such as a clip from *Heroes*, or a song from U2, or a drama based on a *Saturday Night Live* sketch—might make them freak out. Taking them to a church where they can experience the move of God in a service where those elements were used—that puts meat on the bones. That opens hearts and eyes.

You probably don't need to expose your entire church, just your influencers—those who everyone else looks to for their nods of approval. Some of these people are in positions of leadership. Others are just natural leaders who have the respect of many others.

KEYWORD: PLAYPLACE | PopGoesTheChurch.com

Find your influencers and expose them through:

Conferences—Many churches are now offering conferences and would provide good exposure for your leaders. Some are conferences specifically about leveraging the culture, and others are hosted by churches that are getting it done. I have listed several examples in the chapter called *Stuff*.

One caution about conferences: No church is as good as its conference. During a one- or two-day conference, they pull out the best of the best. They don't show you the flops or failures. They typically show you what worked. So don't feel too bad if your church service doesn't stack up to their conference, because theirs doesn't either.

Church Tours—Find a church within a few hours of your location that is leveraging culture well. Rent a bus or convoy in cars and visit one of their services. Seeing another church in action will open eyes and save dozens of hours of trying to explain what you are talking about.

Services by Video or Web Streaming—It might not be practical to get everyone to another church on a Sunday morning, but you could get a DVD of a church service and gather everyone to watch it. Or begin watching portions of services from churches that offer it on the web.[*]

Books—At the risk of looking as if I am pimping[†] my own book, I am going to pimp my own book. Seriously, if this book has you wishing for something different at your church, or you identify with what I've written, then figure out a way to get this in the hands of as many of your leaders as possible. Do a book study with various groups and ask them to read a couple chapters at a time and come in

163

[*] We stream our entire service free every week at GCCWired.com.

[†] To "pimp" something in pop culture vernacular means to "strongly promote or support a certain thing." There you go—I have just launched your pop culture education.

prepared to discuss it. Wrestle with principles you agree with and talk about the stuff you think is heresy.

Guest Speakers—Sometimes an outside speaker can say something in a fresh way or give new insight. One of the best ways to do this is to invite a pastor or leader from another church that is well known for leveraging the culture in their services. Ask him to come and share the story of his church, and make sure he brings many video examples and stories of life change.

Blogs and Podcasts—There are literally hundreds of great resources on the internet that, if carefully selected, can help you further this conversation in your church. Suggesting certain podcasts or blogs from church leaders who are already leveraging the culture will help you continue the dialogue with your leaders. You might start with the companion website for this book—PopGoesTheChurch.com.

LEAD FROM THE MIDDLE

I have never been the top dog. I've never owned a company; I've never been the principal of a school; I have never run a country, been chairman of the board, or been the captain of a sports team. I have always been right in the middle—sometimes toward the bottom of the middle, and sometimes toward the top. Yet I have always had to figure out how to influence people above and around me to change.

Whether you want to change the color of the carpet in the office or you want to see your church begin to leverage pop culture, here are a few things I have picked up along the way that will help you lead from the middle.

Never Stop Learning. There is nothing more annoying than a know-it-all. And when she is right, she is even more annoying. When I have someone come into my office with an attitude of superiority, as though he has been blessed with an extra measure of human intelligence, I don't want to listen to him. He may even have a good point, but my human nature begs me to ignore him. Life-long learners, on the other hand, have a spirit of humility. They are always looking for an opportunity to learn. And so they are able to convince others to change because of their attitude.

Always Add Value. In every interaction, every relationship, every day—look for ways to add value to others, expecting nothing in return. Do this until it becomes as natural as breathing. Never do this for personal gain or to manipulate others, but because it is the right thing to do. You will be amazed how this increases your influence exponentially.

Identify the Influencers. In any group, a few people are the influencers. They are not always the positional leaders. They don't always have a title. But when a new idea is proposed or a change is suggested, all heads turn to look at the one or two influencers to see how they will respond. If they smile and nod their head, the proposal will pass.

> **It is a good idea to identify the influencers and begin meeting them one-on-one. Work through them, not around them.**

If they sit back, cross their arms, and shake their heads, the proposal probably won't go anywhere.

It is a good idea to identify the influencers and begin meeting them one-on-one. Work through them, not around them. Invite them; don't inform them. And make sure you follow the next piece of advice.

Listen Carefully. Few have practiced and far fewer have perfected this true art. Listening takes time. It takes an authentic desire to learn. Listening sometimes requires going past the words to the underlying values. You may think singing the old hymns of faith every week is near and dear to Edna's heart, when listening carefully might unearth a far deeper desire—she wants to feel the presence of God moving like she remembers as a child.

Pay Attention to Timing. My wife is very good at this. She knows there are times to bring things up, and there are days when it just wouldn't be helpful. In an organizational setting, suggesting a change on the wrong day may mean you lose months of progress. You might have to loosen up on your plans a little bit and use some discernment on the right time to pitch your idea.

Share Stories. People are not nearly as interested in *what* you want to change as *why* you want to change it. So link every suggested change back to how it will affect people and how it will help accomplish the purposes of the church. If you are doing something completely new in your church, then share stories of what has happened in other churches when they began to head in that direction. The right stories help reduce negative emotion and increase positive emotion in any major change.

One More Thing. Even those people who you think are in the position of top dog are not really. They have boards to whom they are accountable, deacons or elders to please, and denominational officials who want reports. So cut them some slack and follow the advice of the writer of Hebrews who said, "Be responsive to your pastoral leaders. Listen to their counsel. They are alert to the condition of your lives and work under the strict supervision of God. Contribute to the joy of their leadership, not its drudgery. Why would you want to make things harder for them?"[1] That might mean you will need to honor the local leadership and see your dream of a church fully engaging the culture fulfilled in another location.

BECOME A POP CULTURE EXPERT

If you want to begin to engage the culture in your church, you should start studying the culture. You can't afford to be out of touch with the popular culture that is impacting our communities more than anything else is. When you see that a certain movie is capturing the hearts and minds of the culture, ask the question, "Why?" Figure out what it reveals about the hunger people have in their hearts today for the supernatural or for deeper relationships. When someone has an emotional response to a song, we must explore that. How can we use that to connect with him or her better? When there is a TV show that is a huge success, we need to ask questions, even if the show is based on bad values or it contains inappropriate material. What redemptive analogies can we find to help connect our audience with their core felt needs?

A few ways to do this:

Awards Shows—Watching the *Academy Awards*, the *MTV Movie Awards,* or *The People's Choice Awards* shows can educate you on what is captivating our culture. I recently recorded the *MTV Music Awards*, not because I am crazy about the music or like hearing celebrities talk about what they are wearing, but so I could study how better to leverage our culture. You can get ideas for staging, props, transitional elements, video usage, graphics, and more from these awards shows. Some of our video and music team came over to watch it with me to get ideas for treatments on music videos. Many times, we are creating music videos behind our songs, so seeing what the culture responds to is highly valuable.

Concerts—This past summer, I experienced my first rock concert. I've been to concerts, such as *Jump5* and *ZOEgirl*, with my kids, but I've been told those don't count. When I was younger, I went to several Southern Gospel concerts, but for some reason those don't count either. So five of us jumped in a car and headed to Chicago for a concert featuring *Linkin Park*, *My Chemical Romance,* and eight other bands. The trip was fun, enlightening, and educational. We talked all the way back about things we saw that might help us connect better with the people at Granger.

Entertainment Weekly—This is a magazine that is published weekly, and I always go through it cover to cover. I read the articles to find trends or changing thoughts in the industry to learn how people are responding to the culture. I also look at the Top 20 charts for the highest rated movies, songs, TV shows, and books. I am constantly asking, "How can we leverage what is happening in the culture to reach people for Jesus?"

Music—There is a radio station in just about every region that plays the Top 20 or 40 songs for that local area. You may not find a song you can use in your service, but you will definitely notice issues and topics that are important to the people living around you.

You know what? You don't need to be the expert at this as long as someone on your team is. You may not have the time, energy, or passion to stay tuned into pop culture. That is okay. If you aren't a pop culture expert, just make sure someone on the team is. Pull in people who are spiritu-

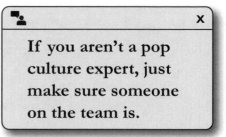

If you aren't a pop culture expert, just make sure someone on the team is.

ally discerning yet think like outsiders—people who have their eyes and ears open to the spiritual topics being raised in the culture.

DON'T CONDEMN THE ART

A caution to the preachers in the crowd: As you begin to pull cultural elements into your service so that you can reach new people, be careful not to be condemning or judgmental. It is a huge bait-and-switch that will backfire if you encourage your congregation to invite their friends to the upcoming, relevant series based on the Beatles music, and then you rail on people who listen to Beatles music.

The Bible is clear that we are not to judge those who are not following Christ. Paul wrote, "What business is it of mine to judge those outside the church? Are you not to judge those inside? God will judge those outside."[2] It will not help the cause of Christ if you invite the community to your church, and then tell them their books are smutty, their shows are immoral, and their music is dishonoring to God. Even if you think some of that should be said to the followers of Christ, it should be done at a different time, and in a different way.

That is why at Granger we have practiced a two-prong approach for the past twelve years. There are principles we teach that are only for followers of Christ, and we present these at a service that is not on the weekend. There are also practices we don't do during the weekend services, such as communion and extended corporate worship, because we think these can be confusing or even a turn-off to the non-believer.

Since Saturday night and Sunday morning are still the culturally acceptable times to attend church in our community, we preserve those services as easy-entry opportunities for the entire community, and we offer a different service during the week, as well as Bible studies and smaller group venues, for our believers who want to take additional steps.

DON'T WORRY ABOUT BEING ORIGINAL

I have met church leaders who refuse to use something that has been used somewhere else. They want to be the first to do something, try something, or preach something.

You can be innovative without being original. Sometimes the most innovative idea for your church or your community is something that was borrowed from somewhere else. That is okay, because being original is overrated.

169

At Granger, we get lots of attention for being innovative. In 2007, we were named the second most innovative church in America.[3] In 2008, we were on the list again in the number three slot. However, here is a secret: Very little of what we do is original. Once or twice a year, we have a good idea that hasn't been done. (At least that is what we think when we do it, but often we find out later that another church did the same thing a few years prior!)

Most of our ideas come from taking someone else's idea and making it work for us. We *Grangerize* it. That is, we make it work for our culture, and that is okay with us. We truly do not care whether what we do is original or not—we just care if it works. If it is effective, who cares whether we got the idea from a church in Dothan or Reno or Tupelo? If we can use the idea to impact our community, why does it matter if it is an already-been-used idea from LifeChurch. tv or Willow Creek?*

I think many churches need to get over themselves and just figure out what works.†

SOME CHRISTIANS SHOULD DISENGAGE FROM THE CULTURE

When Faith and I first were married in 1990, we committed to not owning a television for one entire year. Did we think TV was evil? No. Did we not have enough money to buy one? That wasn't it, and we were actually offered five TV sets in the first year from people who felt sorry for us.

No, for us it was a decision of focus. We were in a brand new life that was unfamiliar to both of us. We were experiencing a new culture together, and we wanted to lay a foundation that would allow

---

* I have included a list of idea sources in the *Stuff* chapter to get you started.

† When you use someone else's idea, don't forget to give them credit.

our marriage not only to survive—but also to thrive. We didn't want anything to get in the way of that goal.

There may be a period in the life of a brand new follower of Christ when he should totally disengage from the culture. It is possible he will need to focus 100 percent on his new life in Jesus. At first, it is not about reaching out to others. It is about laying a good foundation for his new life in Christ. It is possible that any engagement in the culture will pull him back into the choices and lifestyles he is leaving behind. In a sense, he needs to let the pendulum swing far to the other side for a short time while he becomes grounded in this new life. Then, after some time, he can let it swing back in the middle as he figures out what a balanced Christian life looks like.

COPYRIGHT OR COPYWRONG?

I field quite a few questions about the copyright laws and about how they apply to churches. Is it okay to show a TV clip? Is it okay to sing a U2 song? Is it okay to synchronize a popular song to video? Is it okay to make copies of a music CD for the purpose of rehearsal? It seems there are always people who think we aren't doing enough to follow the law, and others who think it's not a big deal and we shouldn't worry about it.

Recently, I had a pleasant e-mail conversation with a man who was considering attending Granger, but he first wanted answers about our policy on copyright adherence. He wanted some specific responses on how we would handle events like showing the Super Bowl or displaying copyright information from licensed material used during services. Here, in part, is what I wrote to him:

Dear Tom,

    I am certain you will find that Granger won't be able to live up to your expectations of copyright

171

compliance. As you know, the law is muddy. Even with the fair use guidelines, there is a lot left to interpretation and to courts to decide. We do everything we can to comply, but we are not attorneys nor do we spend a lot of money on attorneys to keep us in compliance. We want that money invested in ministry. We believe the spirit of the law is not to steal money from the pockets of the artists, producers, or authors who were involved in the work. We are a huge proponent of the arts and those who create it, so that is our heart. Where the law is black and white and we know about it—we do everything we can to comply. Where it is gray or unclear—we interpret it liberally adhering to the spirit of the laws, as we understand them.

If you are selecting a church based on its ongoing copyright compliance and ability to defend every decision made at every level of the church—then I'm going to encourage you to look elsewhere. If you are looking for a place that is run with great intention and high integrity, where true life transformation is happening to hundreds every year, and where the message of Jesus is intertwined with innovative and relevant methods...then keep checking out Granger.

I know that response is probably not politically correct and might come under fire from some who enjoy the *land of legalism* more than I do, but as a recovering card-carrying citizen, I encourage churches to keep their eye on the mission.

If you Google the topic of churches using copyrighted material, you will find some who define it narrowly (you can't use anything without permission) and others who define it liberally (everything is fair game). It is important to pay attention to who is giving the advice. I find many of the people who define the issue very conservatively have something to gain by that view (for example, they are a songwriter, publisher, author, or represent someone who is). It is true there are some black and white rules, but it is also true there is a whole middle ground which is gray and which hasn't been defined by law or by the courts.[*]

An important document to consult is straight from the copyright office of the United States government and is called Section 107.[4] The government has set up this "fair use" section of the copyright law for the specific purpose of allowing certain instances where you can use copyrighted material without permission.

For example, there are two instances cited when you can use a short portion of a show or movie: 1) use in a parody or when some of the content of the work is parodied; and 2) reproduction by a teacher or student of a small part of a work to illustrate a lesson. It might be concluded that the Fair Use Guidelines cover our rewrite of *The Culps* routine from *SNL* as a parody, and our inclusion of a *Desperate Housewives* clip as being used by a teacher for an illustration.

Of course, every church will need to decide for itself how it will interpret the law in order to protect the interests of the church. I'm not a copyright expert or attorney, but following are some very useful tools available to help you stay compliant with the laws that are black and white:[†]

173

---

[*] I have never heard of a church which has been taken to court for these type of copyright issues. I also do not think it would be a good stewardship of time for a church to end up in court fighting a well-financed production house. However, as long as the law is gray, it makes sense to me to interpret it in such a way that we can have a greater impact on our communities.

[†] This is current as I am writing but changes quickly. Check the websites for the most up-to-date services and pricing. In addition, remember that all these organizations make their money through a conservative interpretation of the law.

Christian Copyright License International (ccli.com)—For the use of most worship songs and lyrics used during a service. Cost ranges from $49 to $4,260 per year based on the size of your church.

Performance Rights Organizations—Various groups license churches to perform in public including ASCAP (ascap.com), BMI (bmi.com), and SESAC (sesac.com). If you are a member of the Willow Creek Association (willowcreek.com), you can subscribe to all three of these licenses for $149 with no reporting required.

Church Video Licensing (cvli.org)—For the usage of most video/TV/VHS/DVD clips to show during a service. Annual cost is from $55 to $625 based on church size, with a 10 percent discount for Willow Creek Association members.

WingClips (wingclips.com)—This group gets permission in advance from movie studios, distribution companies, and filmmakers

To run the numbers, purchasing all of the listed licenses, your costs, which include the Willow Creek membership fee, would be as follows:

Church Attendance	CCLI*	BMI, ASCAP & SESAC w/ WCA Membership	CLVI*	WingClips^	Total Annual Cost
200	$223	$149+249	$190	$120	$931
500	$312	$149+249	$265	$120	$1,095
1,000	$382	$149+249	$365	$120	$1,265

*Willow Creek members also get additional discounts through CCLI and CVLI, not represented here.
^WingClips rate assumes paying for an entire year in advance.
All pricing listed here is current as of January 12, 2008, as listed on their respective website.

to use certain scenes from movies, and they often have clips available before the movies have been released. They are free for medium resolution, or for less than $10 a month you can subscribe and have access to their entire high-resolution library.

Of course, you may not want to mess with all of that or you may be in a situation that is more complex. If you want to hire an organization to do everything for you, contact the Church Copyright Administration (churchca.com). They also offer a product called the WorshipCast License for churches that stream their services over the internet (at an annual cost of $995).

These tools are amazingly helpful. At Granger, we subscribe to every available license, submit the reports as they are required, and do what is reasonably possible to comply with the black and white portions of the copyright law.

ENOUGH ABOUT GRANGER

This idea of leveraging pop culture is not a Granger idea. It is not something that uniquely works in our bedroom community outside of South Bend. It is happening all across the United States and around the world. In fact, the chapter I am most excited about in this book is the one that comes next—stories from pastors and churches all across the country who are engaging the culture effectively and uniquely. Turn the page and see if it excites you as much as it does me.

175

chapter 12

TWENTY CHURCHES.
TWENTY STORIES.

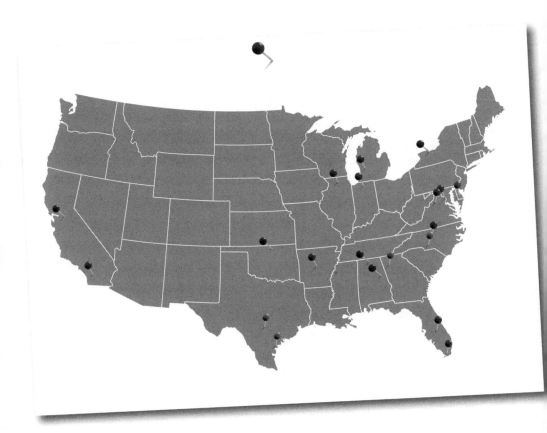

TWENTY CHURCHES. TWENTY STORIES.

Pine Ridge Church, Burlington, NC
Summit Church, Orlando, FL
National Community Church, Washington, D. C.
Bay Area Fellowship, Corpus Christi, TX
Crossroads Grace Community Church, Manteca, CA
Reston Community Church, Reston, VA
Shore Fellowship Church, Egg Harbor Township, NJ
Flamingo Road Church, Miami, FL
Nappanee Missionary Church, Nappanee, IN

Journey Church, Auburn, AL
Oak Leaf Church, Cartersville, GA
Crosspoint Community Church, Decatur, AL
Elevation Church, Charlotte, NC
The Orchard, Aurora, IL
The Summit Church, North Little Rock, AR
North Baptist Church, Rochester, NY
Chorus Church, Murrieta, CA
Enid First Assembly, Enid, OK
The Connection Church, Kyle, TX
Ada Bible Church, Grand Rapids, MI

Enough about theory. Enough about theology. Enough examples from a cornfield in Indiana.

The twenty churches represented in this chapter are diverse. They represent many denominations. Some are rural, some suburban. Some are huge churches and others are very small. Some have been around for decades, and others are only a few weeks old.

Some of these churches are traditional in their style; others are decidedly not traditional. But each of these churches has a story. Although each story is different, they all reflect a leader who is working hard to leverage the culture with a driving passion to help people realize how much they matter to God.

We'll start in North Carolina with one of the more radical churches.

PIMPIN' JESUS

Pine Ridge Church, Burlington, NC
Tadd Grandstaff, Lead Pastor
pineridgechurch.com

Attendance: 275 (after 17 weeks)
Interesting Fact: Started September 2007

In December 2007, the young leaders (oldest staff member is thirty years old) at Pine Ridge launched a series called "XXXChristmas." They decided to expose Christmas for what it really is and was always meant to be. The first week's message was called, "Pimpin' Jesus." They talked about how Christians and the church tend to pimp Jesus during the holidays for their own agendas rather than showing people the love of Jesus. At Pine Ridge, they intentionally open every week with a mainstream song that is picked to tie into the message, and then use that song for a point of reference for the main idea of the day. Tadd Grandstaff says, "We are willing to use whatever means available to reach as many people as we can for Christ, and we intend to use our culture to get it done."

Why use pop culture? "Everything I see on TV, or in a movie, or hear on the radio...I am thinking of a way to use it in a service to capture our generation," adds Tadd. "I think it's so important to use what's out there because it is something people can really relate to. It's something they see or hear every day. I want to open their eyes to their culture and show them how God is a real part of that culture. Now, they can begin to see God in everything."

Results: Over 70 percent of those attending Pine Ridge have never been to church (or haven't been in many years), and most of those are men. Tadd says, "We have so many women come up to us after the services and tell us that they are so excited about our church because they have been trying to get their husbands into church for years and for the first time their husbands are dragging them to church."

Are you just trying to be cool? "We don't incorporate mainstream music, video clips, and series titles just for the heck of it. We don't want to be a church that is trying to be 'cool.' We want everything we do to be very strategic. Everything we do has a purpose and meaning, and it all ties into the overall theme of the series. I think the only danger is when churches begin incorporating elements into their services just for the sake of keeping up with the culture. It's either who you are or it's not. Too many churches are jumping on the pop culture bandwagon and really don't know anything about the culture. But it's important for our generation because for far too long church has been way too boring and way too outdated. By using pop culture, we show how relevant God and the Bible are in our culture today."🖳⁾

> Too many churches are jumping on the pop culture bandwagon and really don't know anything about the culture.

181

🖳⁾ KEYWORD: STORIES | PopGoesTheChurch.com

ICE ICE BABY

Summit Church, Orlando, FL
Isaac Hunter, Senior Pastor
summitconnect.org

Attendance: 1,700
Interesting Fact: They launched in 2002 with twenty-five people just a few miles up the road from Disney World.

Doing church so close to Disney World and Universal Studios brings some unique challenges. It would be asinine if Summit Church tried to compete with these entertainment powerhouses, but they don't even try. Rather than strive to be entertaining, they work on being engaging. This doesn't mean, however, they don't leverage the culture. Isaac Hunter recently taught a three-week series on the Sabbath using the classic lyrics from Vanilla Ice as the title, "Stop, Collaborate, and Listen." People who knew the song remembered the series with ease and hummed the tune to "Ice Ice Baby" for weeks.

Is this example unusual, or do you often tie your series into the culture? "We are more likely to leverage contemporary pop culture in the way Summit looks and feels. For example, we use quarterly magazines rather than traditional newsletters. We also bring in the work of local artists to populate the walls of our building and reinforce the truths of the teaching series."

So pop culture isn't the only tool you use to communicate truth? "I think it is important to use all of life to illustrate God's truth. Pop culture must be used when it's the most helpful method of communication, but high culture should also be on the table. We are always asking, 'What helps us engage people with the Gospel?' and 'What helps us communicate the truth God is calling us to tell, live, and invite others into?'"

Is it important to you to be relevant? "Relevancy is a tool, not an objective; a means and not an end. You can be relevant without being helpful—that's important to remember. Equally important is the reality that the converse is not true. We cannot be helpful without being relevant. We cannot lead people to Jesus if we refuse to meet them where they are, using methods that do not alienate them."

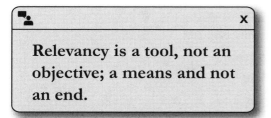

Relevancy is a tool, not an objective; a means and not an end.

Any final thoughts? "Our goal is to engage the people in the culture that surrounds us—not to fight against the culture and not to deify it. Pop culture changes too quickly to make it a good foe or a longstanding friend. It is 'a very good servant, but a very bad master.' The question for Summit is not, 'How can we use pop culture to illustrate truth?' It is, 'What can we do to engage people with the Gospel?' If the most engaging thing we think of comes straight out of the culture that surrounds us, then it would be a sin not to use it."

KEYWORD: STORIES | PopGoesTheChurch.com

GOD @ THE BOX OFFICE

National Community Church, Washington, D. C.
Mark Batterson, Pastor
markbatterson.com
theaterchurch.com

Attendance: 2,000
Interesting Fact: They have eight services at four locations and 73 percent of those who attend are single and in their twenties. Bonus fact: They also operate the largest coffeehouse on Capitol Hill.

Each year, National Community Church (NCC) repeats two series that always end up being the most talked about by regular attendees and guests alike. "God @ the Billboards" is a series where they unpack truth from current music hits, and during "God @ the Box Office," they do the same thing with the biggest movies of the year. Mark Batterson says, "The 60 percent of Americans

> **Sixty percent of Americans who don't attend church get their theology from movies and music.**

who don't attend church get their theology from movies and music. So we redeem popular songs and popular movies by juxtaposing them with scripture. I think of movies and music as idols to an unknown god. They raise spiritual questions and I think we've got answers. So we exegete the movies and juxtapose them with scripture. I love the challenge of redeeming the spiritual themes and pointing people to Christ."

What is one movie you considered in your most recent series?
"*Spider-Man 3*, which is a movie about waging war on your sin nature.

Sin is symbolized by the symbiote that attaches itself to Spider-Man and brings out the worst in him. Sin binds itself to us and turns us into the person we don't want to become. So where do you go when you don't like who you have become? It is symbolized so beautifully in the movie: You go to the Cross. Spider-Man hears the church bells and is transformed beneath the cross."

Why be relevant? "I think of pop culture as Trojan horses. We package the truth in ways to get around people's natural defense mechanism. It is our creativity in redeeming culture that can often earn us a hearing. It's all about incarnation. Jesus was the master of metaphors. He used agricultural metaphors because he lived in an agrarian society. He used culture to incarnate truth."

Can this become a gimmick? "It is very easy for pop culture to result in a watered-down or dumbed-down version of the Gospel. You've got to guard against it. The key is our motivation. If we use pop culture just to be cool, then it'll come across as a gimmick because it is. If we are motivated by our desire to incarnate truth so people can understand God, then it'll come across as authentic. And authenticity is the key. Don't do it because everybody else is doing it. Don't do it because it's the cool thing to do. Do it because you want to preach the truth in terms that people can identify with."

185

KEYWORD: STORIES | PopGoesTheChurch.com

THE HOUSE OF BLUES

Bay Area Fellowship, Corpus Christi, TX
Bil Cornelius, Pastor
bilcornelius.com
bayareafellowship.com

Attendance: 5,500
Interesting Fact: Approximately 50 percent of church is Hispanic

Bay Area Fellowship, located on what is known as the "third coast," did a series on depression, entitled "Leaving the House of Blues." To add to the feel, they hung real electric guitars all around their building and over their stage. If you have ever been to House of Blues in Vegas or Orlando, you would have recognized the way they designed their auditorium stage. The band sang blues music and even adjusted the worship songs to give them a blues feel. Pastor Bil Cornelius began the first message in a straight jacket and talked about feeling as if you are going crazy with depression.

What were the results? Bil says, "Our attendance jumped 1,255 people in a week and over 135 people received Christ during the four-week series. Also, judging by the DVD/CD sales, this series touched people right where they are living."

Why do you engage the culture? "To ignore pop culture, in my opinion, is to ignore the largest opportunity for outreach. Either we can quote dead preachers like Spurgeon (who is awesome, but only preachers even know who he was) or we can quote Oprah, Dr. Phil, Bono, and Kanye West. I'm not comparing their wisdom to Spurgeon, but they are listened to, and we can harness their insights, even when they are wrong, which is often the case."

What about churches that do not use pop culture? "Every church is designed off of the relevance of pop culture. Some are just designed off the pop culture of the 1800s (i.e. Sunday night church was designed to allow farmers to go home in the afternoon and feed their animals and make it back for discipleship time), or the 1950s (i.e. Sunday school was designed to address the growing popularity of suburban schools, so we coined 'Sunday school' to attract suburbanites). Every church is relevant to pop culture; some are just relevant to a pop culture of yesterday. To say you are not concerned with pop culture is to say you are actually stuck in a previous era, and only acting as if that era was 'more holy' than the one we are in now."

> x
>
> **Every church is relevant to pop culture; some are just relevant to a pop culture of yesterday.**

What about criticism? "When being creative, do not react to churches around you that criticize you. When you pull back so you don't go too far for them (or for your most conservative members), you land in 'no man's land.' This is where you are not relevant enough to impress the *unchurched*, yet you are too relevant to impress the 'old guard.' You have to decide your goal: Focus on reaching new people or focus on keeping disgruntled people. You can't do both."

187

KEYWORD: STORIES | PopGoesTheChurch.com

A CAR SHOW AND A BEATLES BAND

Crossroads Grace Community Church, Manteca, CA
Mike Moore, Pastor
crossroadsgrace.org

Attendance: 1,500

Interesting Fact: I had a chance to visit Manteca and meet Mike and his staff at Crossroads Grace Community in November 2007 and found them to be the real deal!

Mike Moore started Crossroads Grace Community twenty years ago in the central valley of California and has always tried to be a student of the culture. In 2006, they offered a series called "Blast to the Past," which included a Vintage Car Show in the parking lot, followed by a Beatles Tribute Band brought in from Los Angeles. Following the concert, Ken Mansfield, former U.S. manager of Apple Records and personal liaison for the Beatles between the U.K. and U.S., shared his story of life with the Beatles and his eventual path to meeting Christ.

> People far from God smell a gimmick and the end result can be worse than no attempt at all.

How did it turn out? Mike says, "There were many people who came to hear the music and meet Ken who had never darkened a church before. Then when they heard the message, wrapped in the language of our culture, they received it well. The real outreach was considered a bridge building opportunity and not an 'in your face' presentation of the Gospel. Ken was compelling and clear in his message of Christ, without coming across as preachy. I believe this is a very effective way to reach people and build the church in today's world. I also believe the systems that are designed to assimilate and grow up believers must be in place to make this model work. Much of the criticism today directed at churches that use pop culture is due to assuming the church is there to simply entertain the culture and not lead them to take their next steps into an authentic life with Christ."

Any cautions? "My only caution is to make sure the message is coming from a place of authenticity. People far from God smell a gimmick and the end result can be worse than no attempt at all. This is a tough one to articulate, but the heart of the caution is to make sure it is designed with a lot of prayer and executed with excellence. The motive behind all pop culture outreach must be at its core a sincere attempt to present the Gospel message in a relevant way."🖳

🖳 KEYWORD: STORIES | PopGoesTheChurch.com

THE WISDOM OF GARRISON KEILLOR

Reston Community Church, Reston, VA
Ben Arment, Pastor
benarment.com
towncenterchurch.com

Interesting Fact: Ben got fed up with church growth conferences, so he dreamed up his own idea of an ideal conference, found sponsors and speakers, and launched his first one in May 2008 called The Whiteboard Sessions (thewhiteboardsessions.com).

Ben and Ainsley Arment started History Church in 2001 in this bedroom community outside Washington, D.C., and then re-launched it as Reston Community Church in the summer of 2007 (he used the internet blog to raise much of the money for the re-launch). In the early 1970s, Reston was one of the first completely planned communities in the country. It was founded on some socially liberal convictions, and so there was no place allotted for churches. Ben and his team have been very creative finding places to meet, and last summer they began to hold services at Reston Town Center, a new urban development.

What does leveraging pop culture look like in your community? "Reston is the most educated city in Virginia, which explains why public radio is the most popular choice for radio listeners," says Pastor Ben Arment. "This community gets their kicks from listening to programs like *A Prairie Home Companion*, *Car Talk,* and *This American Life*. Leveraging pop culture in our community is more in the vein of Garrison Keillor than Kanye West."

Give us a recent example. "In order to speak the language of this culture, we presented a message series called 'Story' which was produced much like a public radio broadcast. We played background audio tracks behind key points in the message to provide emotional impact.

For example, while describing the World War II invasion of Normandy to make a spiritual point about courage, we played the sounds of gunfire and battle effects in the background. While reading a description of heaven from the book of Revelation, we played the soundtrack from *Gladiator*, where Maximus rejoins his murdered family in paradise. It was beautiful."

> **The messages came alive for our people in a multi-sensory way. They laughed. They cried. They sang along.**

How did people respond? "The end result sounded like a highly-produced, live radio show played out each week for our congregation. The messages came alive for our people in a multi-sensory way. They laughed. They cried. They sang along."

KEYWORD: STORIES | PopGoesTheChurch.com

HELL'S KITCHEN

Shore Fellowship Church, Egg Harbor Township, NJ
Tim Chambers, Lead Pastor
timchambersblog.com
shorefellowship.com

Attendance: 1,100

Interesting Fact: Shore Fellowship Church has successfully transitioned from a traditional Baptist Church environment just eight years ago to a cutting edge, technology-enhanced, contemporary worship experience reaching out to the culture in southern New Jersey in a fresh way without compromising the message of the Gospel.

It is common for the team at Shore Fellowship to create a series based on pop culture. They do this through series titles and messages that attract people and give them a platform to teach them truth.

What is one recent example? Lead pastor Tim Chambers talks about a recent series they offered called "Hell's Kitchen: How Spice Racks up Your Life." "In this series, we had a cooking set on stage and each week used a different spice to make a point. For example, we used a bitter spice to talk about bitterness in our lives. This was a very practical series based on the journey of the children of Israel from Egypt to the Promise Land in the book of Exodus. As we explored their time in the wilderness, we saw how their lives were filled with drama and spice. We also explored how to deal with the spice that comes into our lives instead of cooking up recipes for disaster. Each week, we had a recurring character by the name of Lou Lived (which is *devil* spelled backwards) who set up that week's topic."

How do you invite people? "We make use of television, radio, newspaper, billboards, and banners to 'market' these series to the general public. Once we attract people with the sermon series titles, we then have an ability to reach them with the Gospel. Using pop culture as leverage helps us attract people who might not otherwise attend church."

Do you ever come up with an idea you do not end up using? "As we are brainstorming ideas for series, we always ask this question, 'Does this idea have a purpose behind it, or are we only doing it because it is cool or different or shocking?' It's always important to run ideas through the filter of 'Does it reinforce our overall message or does it detract from that message?' Often we come up with ideas (i.e. music, videos, and drama) that on the surface appear to be good, but when we analyze them through these filters, they never make it past the brainstorming meeting."

> Once we attract people with the sermon series titles, we then have an ability to reach them with the Gospel.

193

THE CULTURE ISN'T STUPID

Flamingo Road Church, Miami, FL
Troy Gramling, Lead Pastor
troyandsteph.com
flamingoroadchurch.com

Attendance: 7,500
Interesting Fact: Flamingo Road Church is in an area where 92 percent of the community doesn't go to church.

In the fall of 2006, the team at Flamingo Road came up with a series called "IveScrewedUp.com." It was inspired from a recent campaign by the Catholic Church to get people back to the confessionals. Troy Gramling says, "We created an online, anonymous confessional, where anybody could get things off their chest to God—a God who is big enough to be small enough to meet them through the internet.

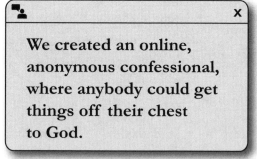

> We created an online, anonymous confessional, where anybody could get things off their chest to God.

During the series, we talked about areas in our lives where we often screw up, such as finances, relationships, faith, and purity."

Did it work? "To our shock, IveScrewedUp.com created a bombardment of local, national, and global media hype. To an even greater alarm, though this series only ran eleven weeks, for eight months after it, we were still receiving media attention (like *USA Today*) and a constant flow of confessors to the online confessional."

Have you done something similar since then? "In September of 2007, we launched another web-based series called

TWENTY CHURCHES. TWENTY STORIES.

"MyNakedPastor.com." We utilized the website to televise a 24/7 webcam that followed me for five weeks, capturing the good, the bad and the ugly. Each week, we tackled real-life subjects that I 'bared' each week, including I Fight, I Get Angry, and I'm Tired. During the first week of the series, our attendance jumped by 1,000 people!"

Why is it so important to build a series around pop culture? "Jesus was very intentional about fusing the Gospel with the current times. Utilizing pop culture creates a common denominator that the church can have with the loss without compromising the truth."

Any final thoughts? "Don't create a series just for the sake of pop culture. The culture can tell—they're not stupid. It's never worth it if it seems pop-cool to us, but seems inauthentic to them."🖥⁾

🖥⁾ KEYWORD: STORIES | PopGoesTheChurch.com

POP AMISH CULTURE

Nappanee Missionary Church, Nappanee, IN
Dave Engbrecht, Senior Pastor
nmconline.net

Attendance: 3,000

Interesting Fact: If you have ever been to Nappanee, Indiana, you have probably been shocked to see a huge church campus on the north end of town, where the weekly attendance equals half the town's population.

Nappanee is a community where you slow down for horse-drawn buggies on your way to church, and where the town theme is "Embrace the Pace." In other words—get used to a slow way of life. So embracing pop culture looks a lot different here than it does in many places. Pastor Dave Engbrecht does not deliver many pop culture-inspired series but does utilize illustrations in his messages to help con-

> **While I want to avoid endorsing all of pop culture, I am willing to use appropriate parts of it to leverage God's truth.**

nect and make a point. He says, "Recently, I expanded on a point by talking about the popular TV show, *Are You Smarter than a Fifth Grader?* I shared my disdain for the program because it exposes my low level of intelligence. Kind of like Mary, in her response to the angel 'gets it' while Zechariah the older and 'wiser' priest doesn't get it. Sometimes the spiritual fifth graders get it while the older more experienced ones in the journey don't."

Do these illustrations work? "I do find a connection with the audience. Using pop culture provides a window during a message that ties people back into the presentation. I think it's important to use the interest points of the audience in our attempt to connect truth. While I want to avoid endorsing all of pop culture, I am willing to use appropriate parts of it to leverage God's truth."

What should churches avoid? "Don't be cute for cute's sake. Sometimes as communicators, it is tempting to be cute instead of effective. Also, make sure the illustration is not bigger than the point that is being made. While we bait the hook to catch the fish, our purpose is not to just display good-looking bait. Our purpose is catching the fish. If people remember the illustration but don't have a clue about the application—I know I've failed miserably."

197

KEYWORD: STORIES | PopGoesTheChurch.com

DEALING WITH THE
CHRISTIAN SUBCULTURE

Journey Church, Auburn, AL
Eric Taylor, Lead Pastor
erictaylor.typepad.com
journeytogether.net

Attendance: 75

Interesting Fact: Journey is a new church plant located near Auburn University.

Do you think it is important to leverage pop culture? Pastor Eric Taylor says, "Absolutely! We have long tried to keep separate the 'secular' and the 'sacred.' As a result, we have created a Christian subculture that has the world's version of everything: Christian clothes, Christian music, Christian books, Christian movies, Christian celebrities, even Christian mints. (Have you heard of Testa-Mints? I think they're supposed to make your breath smell more spiritual or something.) We have isolated and insulated ourselves from the very people Jesus called us to reach. People in the real world see the church in its holy huddle trying to invite THEM (disconnected, far from God) to change to become like US (Christians)."

Why does that bother you? "Because the message of the Gospel was *incarnational*—Jesus went to where the people were. That's our call as well: Go to where they are. That is the Great Commission! Paul also modeled that in Acts 17 as he talked to the Areopagus. He used their own cultural icons as a beginning point to teach them truth."

Why does that matter today? "We are in a culture where you can get Britney, Lindsay, and Paris updates instantaneously on your computer or cell phones, and where kids know more about the cast of *High School Musical* than they do about the twelve apostles. If we are going to be effective in reaching this world that has gone pop culture crazy, then it is imperative that we use pop culture as a bridge to deliver the life-changing message of Jesus in a package they are used to."

What are some recent examples from Journey Church? "One interesting series we did was "Google: The Search Engine for Authentic Relationships." We used the popularity of the internet search engine to drive our graphics and our messages. Also, we began 2008 with "LifeHD," a very basic expositional series on the Sermon on the Mount built around this big idea—Jesus came to show us life in high definition, to help us see everything in a higher resolution, sharper focus, and clearer than ever."

> We have isolated and insulated ourselves from the very people Jesus called us to reach.

Is it possible to go too far? "I have made the mistake before and must always be very careful not to get so wrapped up in pop culture (trying to make the illustrations and stories fit my message or the series) that I forget my primary purpose is to teach truth for life change. If lives aren't being changed, we have to ask ourselves, are we just one more pop culture outlet?"

199

KEYWORD: STORIES | PopGoesTheChurch.com

A LITTLE BIT COUNTRY

Oak Leaf Church, Cartersville, GA
Michael Lukaszewski, Lead Pastor
youcanknowgod.com
oakleafchurch.com

Attendance: 850
Interesting Fact: Oak Leaf was launched in mid-2006 in a small town north of Atlanta, and it has grown very quickly.

Oak Leaf often builds a series around popular music, movies, or other pop culture images. They recently did a series called "Oak Leaf Country," and used popular country songs to help teach their five foundational values. In another message about homosexuality, they used a clip from *The Office* to illustrate a point. In the fall of 2007, they offered a series called "The Games of Life," using popular board games to teach spiritual truths. For example, "Monopoly" was about recognizing that all your money belongs to God.

What were the results? Lead pastor Michael Lukaszewski says, "These messages are some of our most liked throughout the year. Attendance is good, and since our small groups also follow the theme of the weekend message, our small group members seem to be able to talk about the topic a little easier."

Why do you think it is important to pull in pop culture illustrations or to build a message series around a pop culture topic? "Our people need to know we're living in the world and can relate to their lives. I think it's important for attendees to see pastors talking (in person and from the stage) about things they talk about at school and work. It helps us be relatable."

Is it always about relevance? "We have to make sure we are keeping the purpose in mind. The intent is not to be cute or relevant, or to be culturally relevant just for culture's sake. It is a much deeper purpose. I've seen creative ideas that were great ideas but didn't really connect with any scriptural truth."

Are you ever criticized? "We're the church in town that does some mailouts, and the images and words on these cards get labeled as 'provocative.' Or we get accused of going for shock value because we created a website called "yourgreat-sexlife.com." The fact is, our series are designed to attract people that don't go to church—not Christians. The only people that call and complain are Christians. Sure, our mailouts may be a little provocative, but isn't that the point of advertising? We're talking about life, faith, and the Bible, and we want people to come hear it, so why would we want to send out a postcard that DOESN'T get noticed? It's sad that when a church does what a church is called to do, people think it is out of the ordinary. We're not going to tone things down any more than we're going to water things down."🖥️

> Our series are designed to attract people that don't go to church—not Christians. The only people that call and complain are Christians.

201

🖥️ KEYWORD: STORIES | PopGoesTheChurch.com

TOO PROVOCATIVE

Crosspoint Community Church, Decatur, AL
David Anderson, Lead Pastor
moviepastor.com
decaturmoviechurch.com

Attendance: 130

Interesting Fact: Dave's world was rocked at the *Innovate* conference in late 2006. After a challenge from Mark Beeson, he decided he was going to drop his side job and focus on his church full-time, which is what he did in February 2007.

Crosspoint changed locations to a movie theater early in the summer of 2007, shortly after the well-known launch of the iPhone. To promote the move, they distributed ten thousand door hangers promoting a series called "iLIFE." The door hanger graphics used a very slick iPhone theme on one side and an invitation

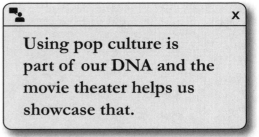

Using pop culture is part of our DNA and the movie theater helps us showcase that.

to the church on the other side. During the series, they gave away an iPod as part of a random drawing during each service. Additionally, they integrated the graphics on the stage and developed a transitional video based on the highly popular iPhone commercials.

What were the results? David Anderson reports, "Average attendance during the series was about 25 percent higher than prior to the series, and several new families connected with our church and are now involved in the ministry."

Have you always worked pop culture into your messages?
"We started in 2002 in a living room with six people. We grew to about 100 in a rented daycare before we moved to the theater. Using pop culture is part of our DNA and the theater helps us showcase that. During the Christmas season in 2007, we launched a series called "Christmas in the REEL World" where we used themes from recent films to talk about the coming of Jesus. We even used non-Christmas movies like *Spider-Man 3* (about forgiveness), *Evan Almighty* (about trusting God), and *Transformers* (about changing the world)."

If a series works at one church, is it guaranteed to work at another church? "Not necessarily. We did a series on the topic of sex, and while the teaching was needed, the advertising we did for it (two billboards) didn't increase attendance at all. Our town is very conservative and "over-churched" and the billboards did not generate much traffic to our web site. We were quite surprised by that. It was probably too provocative."

203

KEYWORD: STORIES | PopGoesTheChurch.com

LOVERBOY AND AC/DC

Elevation Church, Charlotte, NC
Chunks Corbett, Executive Pastor
stevenfurtick.com
elevationchurch.org

Attendance: 2,900 (after 23 months!)
Interesting Fact: Lead Pastor Steven Furtick was born in 1980. (Boy! do I feel old.)

Elevation Church is no stranger to culturally relevant series. One recent example of leveraging pop culture to reach people for Christ was a sermon series based on '80s rock. The series title was "Everything I Need to Know about Elevation Church, I Learned from '80s Rock." It was a series that focused on the four core participation values of the church. Each week, the band performed an '80s song that tied into the sermon. For example, Loverboy's "Working for the Weekend" was played during the week which focused on volunteering, and AC/DC's "Money Talks" was the cover song the week they tackled the topic of stewardship and giving.

How did you invite people to the series? Executive Pastor Chunks Corbett answers, "Since 85 percent of the people that attend Elevation do so after a personal invite, we give everyone something tangible to hand to a friend when they are inviting them to a new series at Elevation. For the '80s rock series, we gave away cassette tapes with a custom printed insert that included an invitation to the series."

Did people come? "We had a 15 percent increase in our attendance the first week of the '80s Rock series (including a 50 percent increase in first-time guests). During the entire four week series, there were 585 first-time adult visitors."

Update: During a January 2008 series called "Made" using a mafia theme, Elevation saw a 1,000-person spike in the first week and retained 800 of them for week two!

Should every church leverage pop culture? "Pop culture has a definite place in any church that intends to reach the *unchurched*. The church today has a lot more to compete with than they did in the '50s. We are competing with the NFL, family time (generally an excuse to be lazy), the bed, and TV. The church is also competing for the workaholic's attention on potentially their only day off.

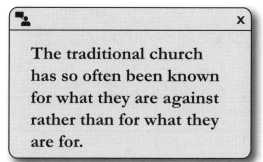

The traditional church has so often been known for what they are against rather than what they are for. This has often been a revolt against pop culture, which has caused a greater divide between the church and culture. When a church leverages pop culture and actually pulls out the good and addresses the topics that face our generation head on, this bridges that gap."

Any final thoughts? "I would challenge churches to become more than just imitators of pop culture. Take pop culture and make it better. When the church imitates pop culture with no innovation, the church assumes its customary backseat to what is relevant and becomes nothing more than a copycat."

205

KEYWORD: STORIES | PopGoesTheChurch.com

A STARBUCKS-ADDICTED PASTOR

The Orchard, Aurora, IL
Scott Hodge, Lead Pastor
scotthodge.org
orchardvalleyonline.com

Attendance: 900

Interesting Fact: The Orchard is an eighty-year-old church community with an intriguing story of how God took a struggling, dying church and led them through a painful, yet rewarding journey of cultural change and transition.

For Easter 2007, the leaders at The Orchard launched a series called "Confessions of a blue jean wearin', Starbucks-addicted pastor." The promotional card read, "There's something refreshing about 'coming clean' and living a life of authenticity and freedom." Later in 2007, they did a series called "Suburban Myths: Uncovering the Truth about Life in the Suburbs." For each of these series, they sent a mailer to the 25,000 homes in the community surrounding the church.

How did it go? Lead pastor Scott Hodge says, "The results were outstanding! During the "Suburban Myths" series, we saw a 30 percent jump in attendance in one week, which has continued to sustain."

Why is it important to leverage pop culture in your series? "Drawing in familiar elements that help tear down walls and defenses in people's minds and hearts is essential—especially since the message of Jesus is not always an easy message to swallow. Using popular music and themes that pull in pop culture helps pave the way for speaking challenging messages into people's lives."

How do we remain faithful while being relevant? After considering this question in *Prophetic Untimeliness: A Challenge to the Idol* *of Relevance*,[1] a book written by Os Guiness, Scott wrote on his blog, "I walk away from reading the book more convinced than ever that the Orchard is on track with the mission God has given us. Do we have it all figured out or perfected? Hardly. But it's right. And I am 100 percent certain that it's worth pouring our lives into. I'm also walking away even further determined to be relevant—even more committed to using creative and innovative ways to share the story of God with a culture that desperately needs to hear it.

> Drawing in familiar elements…is essential—especially since the message of Jesus is not always an easy message to swallow.

But I also walk away from it feeling a tension in my heart. And to tell you the truth, I'm glad I feel it. I would rather be committed to reaching our culture and constantly trying to find the balance in how we do it than having no struggle at all."

KEYWORD: STORIES | PopGoesTheChurch.com

SWIMMING WITH MADONNA

The Summit Church, North Little Rock, AR
Danny Jones, Equipping Pastor
thesummitchurch.org

Attendance: 1,100

Interesting Fact: Danny Jones joined the staff team at the Summit in the summer of 2007. Prior to that, he spent fifteen years building Kompas in Zilina, Slovakia—a training center with the purpose of influencing next-generation church leaders. Capturing and leveraging pop culture was at the core of his strategy in Eastern Europe.

Danny is passionate about using the culture to reach this generation. He says, "I am very convinced that pop culture is one of the most effective tools that God can use to engage a generation that has been anesthetized and is sleeping soundly. I am convinced that all truth is

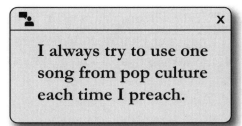

I always try to use one song from pop culture each time I preach.

from God, regardless of the source, or the source's understanding of how he or she is the mouthpiece of God."

Do you see support for this in scripture? "There are many biblical examples—Cyrus and Caiaphas, to name two. I think Jesus' continued connection to culture was what made him both a compelling enigma to the hurting and hungry and an enemy to the aristocracy of the status quo."

Why are you so passionate about this? "For me, it is a part of the redemptive mission of the church. We are redeeming that which the enemy has taken through deception. This includes truth in any context. I find that the shock effect of "redeeming" different aspects of familiar pop culture, and identifying the truth that lies there waiting to be uncovered, awakens this generation of sleepers and suddenly calls them—in a church service of all places—to a confrontation with a reality they didn't expect."

Give us an example. "I do this primarily through music. Music gives me extra miles for my efforts because not only am I engaging my audience on an intellectual level with the truth found in the message, but also on an emotional and relational level, since the greatest power of music lies in those two levels.

In order to accomplish this, I always try to use one song from pop culture each time I preach. Recently, I have used "Waiting for the World to Change" (John Mayer), "Feel" (Robbie Williams), and "You've Got a Friend" (James Taylor) to help the Summit Church understand who we are as a missional community."

Did I hear you have also used Madonna? "Yes. Madonna has helped me immensely through the years with her compelling words and music. A number of students at one youth camp in Slovakia found grace and were set free from the guilt of sin through the words of "Swim." The redemptive analogies in all of pop music are some of the most powerful, yet unused, tools in the church today. I plan to use them as long as they are effective."

KEYWORD: STORIES | PopGoesTheChurch.com

THE GUY FROM THE EXPLOSION

North Baptist Church, Rochester, NY
David Whiting, Senior Pastor
northbaptistchurch.org

Attendance: 600

Interesting Fact: North Baptist is a 120-year-old congregation in transition. Seven years ago, the church decided they wanted to change and begin reaching people far from God. Since then, they have doubled in size.

How have you leveraged culture to make a difference? "We are a video-based culture. I've sat in large auditoriums and found myself sitting close to the front but still watching the screen. So we use video as much as possible. At least once a month, we share stories of dramatic life change by video. We could do a live testimony or a live question-and-answer format, but sharing the story on video keeps everyone's attention."

Do you ever reference TV shows? "In 2007, I preached through the book of Colossians, including a six-week series called 'Relationships 101.' We used hilarious clips from the TV show *Everybody Loves Raymond* to show how not to live. They were purely funny clips and had no purpose but to draw people into the topic. The response from new people was huge. They actually made comments like, 'I never realized the Bible was that practical.'"

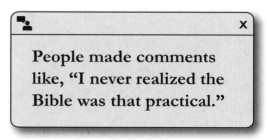

People made comments like, "I never realized the Bible was that practical."

Your church has a traditional history. Do people ever get mad? "After I used the clips from *Everybody Loves Raymond*, there was one church member who watched nineteen episodes and shared with me all of the sexually inappropriate themes that they saw."

How do people respond? "I just heard a story today of a new family who said their children love the videos we show and hearing the 'funny' pastor. Their parents (who don't attend our church) said, 'See, your children just go to church because they are entertained.' The mother responded, 'If the church uses entertainment to teach my children about God and to help them know and love God, then I'm thankful for it.'"

Should every church use pop culture illustrations? "I don't know if I would say it is crucial. There are some great churches accomplishing the Great Commission without using pop culture. But for us, it is very strategic. I just think utilizing illustrations that people relate to just makes sense."

Is the story Tim told about you, him, and the explosion (in the introduction) a true story? "Yep, absolutely true."⌨

211

⌨ KEYWORD: STORIES | PopGoesTheChurch.com

THE CASE OF THE DISAPPEARING DRUMS

Chorus Church, Murrieta, CA
Eric Beeman, Associate Pastor
choruschurch.com

Attendance: 300

Interesting Fact: Murrieta is a suburb of San Diego, Orange County, and Los Angeles. It is one of the fastest growing communities in the nation and has been called the "Bible Belt of Southern California."

Eric Beeman is no stranger to rental facilities and church planting. He was one of the founding pastors at Life Church in Temecula, California, which grew within two years to be listed as one of the fastest growing churches in America. He joined the staff of Chorus Church in 2007, and he is passionate about doing ministry that works.

When did you learn that it is important to leverage the culture to reach people? "Several years ago as a public school teacher. I realized very quickly that students learn better, when you speak in their language. I believe people will learn and grow more quickly when we speak in the language they use every day—pop culture. Missionaries work hard to learn the language and the culture of the country they are being

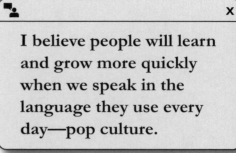

> I believe people will learn and grow more quickly when we speak in the language they use every day—pop culture.

sent to in an effort to better minister to its inhabitants. Why shouldn't we learn and use the language and culture of the community we are called to?"

You oversee several areas at Chorus Church, including worship, media arts, and youth. How are you able to engage the culture from your position? "I'm in the process of bringing our church up-to-date in terms of cultural relevance. I redesigned the staging and projection in the auditorium. We brought in a live drum kit (making the electric kit disappear), and I have slowly been updating the style of music. We'll be launching our new flash-based website in a few weeks."

Are there any limits? "My caution would be not to allow the culture to change the message or cause you to compromise your integrity. For example, just because our culture values sex and drug usage doesn't mean that we should engage in the use of them. But we also shouldn't be afraid to talk about those issues in church." 🖥))

213

🖥)) KEYWORD: STORIES | PopGoesTheChurch.com

A REVOLVING DOOR

Enid First Assembly, Enid, OK
BJ Barrick, Saturday Night Service Pastor
bjbarrick.com
enidfirstassembly.com

Attendance: 700
Interesting Fact: They have four services, each with a unique flavor and name: the Classic Service, the Contemporary Service, the Worship Experience, and the Saturday Night Service. They have grown from 175 to 700 in just a few years.

Half of the town in Enid, Oklahoma is military. They train for ten months and then they are gone. That presents some unique challenges for BJ and the rest of the team. It is like a revolving door. They have to start over every couple of months as some come and some leave. However, they look at it as a way to influence the world. Every week, hundreds of Air Force students are listening to their podcasts from all over the world.

They leverage pop culture throughout the year and believe it is especially important with so many different people from various parts of the country. Once each year, BJ hosts a film festival at the service for young adults.

What does this look like? "We re-live the best in-house videos that we produced from the past year. At our most recent film festival, we had music videos from Nickelback and Tim McGraw, commercial parodies from Sonic, all kinds of music from every decade, clips from *American Idol* and *America's Funniest Home Videos*, HP commercials, relevant news stories, and more."

It looks like you refer to pop culture quite often. "True. There are two elements that we incorporate into every weekend service: stories and cultural relevance. These are a must for success! It's not just important—it's essential. The church, for the most part, has become outdated, irrelevant, archaic, and boring. A huge paradigm shift is needed and is coming!"

> There are two elements that we incorporate into every weekend service: stories and cultural relevance.

So you look for topics to teach out of pop culture? "No. I think it is a mistake to try to build messages around pop culture. Instead, use culturally relevant elements to drive your message. I don't ever want to get to the place where I am trying to find scriptures to relate with the topic. Instead, I want topics to reinforce the scripture."

215

KEYWORD: STORIES | PopGoesTheChurch.com

ACCIDENTAL PROFANITY

The Connection Church, Kyle, TX
Cole Phillips, Lead Pastor
makingtheconnection.org
theconnectionchurch.org

Attendance: 500

Interesting Fact: The Austin suburb of Kyle that had a population of only 2,225 residents in 1990 now boasts a 328 percent growth rate to the current population of 35,000.

Austin is a city that stands in sharp contrast to its Bible Belt surroundings with only 44 percent of the people claiming any connection to a local church. For Pastor Cole Phillips, using pop culture to teach eternal truth started when he was a teenager employing lyrics from Michael Jackson's "Man in the Mirror" and showing clips from *Flatliners* to illustrate forgiveness to other students.

How do you see your role as a missionary to the culture? "The Connection Church is intentional about helping *unchurched* people in the region make the connection between the world they live in everyday and the spiritual principles in God's Word. Cole says, "I see myself as an ambassador from the church to the real world, presenting the Gospel in simple terms that people can own and apply. The real question is, 'How much do I believe lost people matter to God?' If I whole-heartedly believe that, then I have to care about their interests, what's shaping their souls, and the source of their values, which in most cases is pop culture."

How have you used pop culture in the church and what were the results? "NASCAR is huge in Texas, so it was a no-brainer to leverage that theme for the series "DRIVEN." It attracted many racing fans who previously had no interest in God's plan for their lives. Since you're more likely to notice things that you care deeply about, just seeing a stockcar on a piece of direct mail is enough to capture the attention of someone on the lookout for NASCAR. We even brought up an actual stockcar from the local track so people could get up close with the sport."

Do you think it is important to pull in pop culture illustrations or to build a message series around a pop culture topic? "We believe it's a sin to take the most earth-shaking message on the planet and make it boring. Some people have said that you shouldn't take something people are talking about and teach on that. Rather, that you should first choose a Bible passage to teach. However, Jesus didn't teach that way. He regularly used teachable moments to drive God's truth home in powerful ways. When a topic is being addressed in pop culture, the church is given a window to address that issue.

"In the summer, we usually do a message series called *God on Film* (godonfilm.net). Every summer, Hollywood spends tons of money to advertise those summer blockbusters, and we just piggyback on that advertising. Traditionally, churches see a sharp decline in attendance during the summer months. However, we've been able to grow through the summer each year with this strategy. During *God on Film* we also send every first time guest a free movie rental ticket to say thanks for checking out the church."

Do you have any cautions for churches to consider when weaving in pop culture illustrations to a service? "Definitely! If you're playing a recording of a song behind a video, be sure to do a check of the lyrics. We once accidentally used a portion of a classic rock song that had profanity in it that we couldn't hear, but someone in the audience let us know it was there. Oops!"🖳⁾

🖳⁾ KEYWORD: STORIES | PopGoesTheChurch.com

GET'CHA HEAD IN THE GAME

Ada Bible Church, Grand Rapids, MI
Daniel Scott, Children's Ministry Creative Director
adabible.org

Attendance: 5,200

Interesting Fact: Ada is a suburb of Grand Rapids—known as the northern Bible Belt. Nearby are several Christian publishing companies, four Christian colleges, and a church on every corner. But there are still 75,000 *unchurched* families on the east side near Ada Bible Church.

Some might believe that leveraging pop culture doesn't translate to children's ministry. Why would you want to expose kids to what is happening in the culture? But Dan Scott knows they are already exposed to the culture every day, and he uses that knowledge to reach families.

How do you leverage pop culture to help kids or their parents? "We find that parents are often uneducated or unaware of the pop culture their kids are experiencing, so we offer a parenting class called *Pop Culture 101*. In this class, we intentionally do not dismiss pop culture or spend all our time warning about the dangers of the culture. Rather, we want parents to leave with tools for engaging their kids in meaningful conversation about what they are watching, hearing, and experiencing through pop culture."

What about with the kids? Do you think it is important to leverage the culture when teaching them? "Today's kids identify with artists like Hannah Montana and *High School Musical*. When we use a video clip or a soundtrack from these singers, it creates an inviting space for kids to feel comfortable in bringing their friends. I can remember one visitor telling his friend, 'Your church is so cool! You played "Get'cha Head in the Game" from *High School Musical.* Can I come back with you next week?'"

How do you find good pop culture illustrations to use when teaching? "Leveraging pop culture for children is not easy. It takes

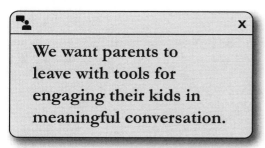

We want parents to leave with tools for engaging their kids in meaningful conversation.

dedicated leaders listening to top 40 radio stations and the top songs downloaded on iTunes. Others are watching MTV, Nick, and Disney, and viewing the latest films that are popular with the kids. There is so much good out there, but it takes time to find it. But when you do, nine times out of ten you end up with a win."

Are there any boundaries? Where do you draw the line? "When we use a song or scene from a movie—we know the kids might later download the entire CD or watch the whole movie. Although it might be a great movie clip to teach a lesson, it also might lead that child to another part of the movie that isn't so great. So we just find another example. We always show discernment for the sake of the kids. If you look hard enough, another great example from pop culture will surface."

219

KEYWORD: STORIES | PopGoesTheChurch.com

chapter 13

SO THAT...

Why?

Why take the time to learn about the culture? Why listen to hits on your iPod or go to the latest blockbuster at the theater? Why spend money on lights, haze, and video screens? Why expend the energy to program an experience rather than just to preach a message?

Why do this through the local church at all? Why tolerate the pain and trauma of a growing church with staff problems and building issues when I can just meet with ten of my friends in a home? Why try to convince my friend to come to church when there is a risk he might be embarrassed? Why continue to trust organized religion when so many leaders have failed?

Why drive so close to the line? Why not tell people to stay as far away from pop culture as possible? There is enough about God in the Bible—why tell them to look for God in the culture?

Why not just let the church be for Christians and figure out ways to reach people outside the church? What is so wrong with wanting a place where we can be with other Christians, study the Bible, and worship God without having to censor our language for seekers?

Let's say all this works and churches begin to leverage pop culture and more people start going to church than ever before.

So what? Who cares? I know I don't. More people mean more cars, more kids, more trash, more strain on the facility, more counseling, more hospital visits, more relational conflict, more letters from unhappy church members, more chances that a leader will mess up, more opinions, more responsibility, and more expectation.

Is that the goal? Do we just want to fill up our previously empty church pews with more warm bodies? Do we do this so our pastors can blog about how many people came to church last weekend? Are we relevant, innovative, and culturally savvy so our church ends up on some top 20 list? Do we just want to be labeled as hip, cool, innovative, or cutting-edge?

I sure hope not. If we are doing all this just to build attendance, we have failed. If the only thing that happens after your church begins leveraging pop culture is a stylishly dressed pastor teaching to a packed building on Sunday morning—that would be a catastrophe.

I probably get this question every week, "How many people are in your church?" Even though we had 6,800 in attendance last weekend (as I write in January 2008), the real answer is probably around 3,500. That is because a crowd is not a church. We may have 6,800 in the crowd every single weekend, but that does not mean we have 6,800 people in the church. The crowd includes the church, but also includes the friends and neighbors they invited. It includes a whole bunch of people just kicking the tires of this thing we call Christianity. It includes some believers who have decided to just ride the waves and not make a commitment to do anything but take up space.

Don't get me wrong. I want as big a crowd as possible. But our goal is to turn the crowd into a church. So we approach every service asking what we can do to help people take steps beyond the weekend experience. How can we get them into a relationship with another follower of Christ? How can we motivate them to buy a Bible and begin to study it? How can we encourage them to attend a study with their spouses so they can begin to make good choices in their marriages? How can we inspire them to join us downtown to help the needy?

We don't want to build an inspiration station where people come week after week, sit, soak, and leave being no different from when they walked in. The Bible tells us that this is like a person who looks in a mirror and does nothing about what they see.[1]

So what is this all about? Why leverage the culture?

That is the question: "Why?"

The answer is simple: "So that…"

So that the man losing his second marriage will find strength from God to be a man that keeps his promises and leads his family. So that the lonely single mom with out-of-control kids will keep her eyes focused on Jesus and be surrounded by other moms doing the same. So that the elderly woman who finds no reason to live will again realize how precious she is to God and will find that purpose for life through helping others.

So that the sexually abused teen will be surrounded by men of God who will help instill in him the confidence to forgive his abusers

Joe,

What do you think? If you knew of a church like the one I'm describing, would you check it out? If this doesn't work to reach you, we've missed the point.

I want to leverage the culture so that you have a safe place to explore your faith; where you can hide until you are ready to be seen; where you will be challenged but not pushed; where you will be loved but not smothered; where you can start where you are, rather than where someone thinks you should be; where you can be in relationship with others without having to make a commitment; where you can ask heretical questions and get authentic answers.

The church should be a place where you know others and you are known, where you love others and you are loved, where you celebrate the steps of others and you are celebrated when you are ready to take yours. That is my hope and dream for you, that you will find such a place.

Thanks for the conversation, Joe.

-Tim

and discontinue the cycle of destruction. So that the couple whose daughters continually make bad choices will find the wisdom to lead their family and the humility to ask others for help. So that the woman who has never experienced acceptance outside of a one-night stand will begin to fully hear and know how her true beauty is being shaped on the inside.

So that the man steeped in years of religious legalism will begin to experience the grace and love of Jesus. So that the woman who has gone to Mass every day for years, but never had a relationship with God, will begin to see her religious activity as an outpouring of love rather than duty.

So that all of these people, and thousands others just like them, begin to take a step toward Jesus. Not the same step; not at the same time; not at the same pace—but that each continues to take his or her next step toward Christ.

So that as they take steps and find help and hope in the church, they will begin to serve the poor. They will begin to use their God-given abilities and resources to tackle the biggest issues in their communities—problems such as crime, teen pregnancies, and the failure of the educational system. So by gaining strength in their new life based on the Word of God, they will draw on that strength to make a difference in the world. They will begin to pray more, serve more, love more, give more, extend grace more, forgive more, value others more, and help more—in the church, yes, but also in the schools, colleges, homes, factories, offices, stores, fields, and streets of the community.

I began this book by writing, "Where is the impact of the church? Where is the church that has an impact so loud it can't be denied by the community?"

The answer, I hope, is in your community. That is my prayer.

STUFF TO READ, CLICK, VIEW
AND CHECK OUT

My first three books all had the word "stuff" in the title, so it seems appropriate that I would at least use that word in a chapter title. Some might call this an "appendix," but it never made sense to me to name a chapter after a useless body part that tends to kill people when it becomes infected.

My goal in the next several pages is to load you up with resources that will help you leverage the culture in your local church.

BOOKS 💻))

A Matrix of Meanings: Finding God in Pop Culture by Craig Detweiler and Barry Taylor. Rather than getting upset at the culture for the way it is taking down the country, Craig and Barry see God's fingerprints as they look around. They see a search for spiritual meaning in places you would not expect. They are pastors, teachers, and seminary graduates, as well as pop culture fans. They weave scripture through the book as they put a spotlight on God in the culture. They take 350 pages to do what I tried to do in just a few in chapter six.

Christ and Culture by Richard Niebuhr. This is evidently a classic because at least twenty of my reviewers indicated that *Pop Goes the Church* was a modern-day version of this 1956 work. I'll admit I had never heard of the title or the author, but after several recommendations, it would seem strange not to include it in this list. I'm planning to get a copy and read it myself.

Eyes Wide Open: Looking for God in Popular Culture by William D. Romanowski. Bill is a professor at Calvin College, and so writes like an academician (which means some of it is over my head), but this book is crammed full of great insight. He urges us to view music and

💻)) KEYWORD: STUFF | PopGoesTheChurch.com

movies as thoughtful critics who are wide-awake to both the good and the bad. Bill first wrote this book in 2001, but make sure you pick up a copy of the "revised and expanded edition" that was published in 2007.

Faith, God, and Rock & Roll: From Bono to Jars of Clay, How People of Faith are Transforming American Popular Music by Mark Joseph. He should get some attention for having the longest title. Mark documents a recent shift as Christian artists and Christian groups have abandoned the Christian music subculture and resurfaced at mainstream record labels. He looks at the impact groups such as Lifehouse, Switchfoot, P.O.D., and Collective Soul are having on the culture.

How Movies Helped Save My Soul: Finding Spiritual Fingerprints in Culturally Significant Films by Gareth Higgins. The author believes there is more to going to movies than just mindless entertainment. With chapters on fear, God, justice, love, power and more, Higgins teaches how to make sense of the spiritual by looking at films with a new perspective and includes an analysis of *The Matrix, Magnolia, Fight Club, Field of Dreams,* and more than two hundred other films.

Jack Bauer's Having a Bad Day by Tim Wesemann. I must admit, *24* is one of my favorite TV shows. Who wouldn't want to be Jack Bauer for just one day? This book is a great example of how you can take a pop culture phenomenon, such as the show *24*, and use it to teach spiritual truths. Wesemann unlocks, you guessed it, twenty-four different spiritual truths about faith in God and even includes a small group study guide in the back of the book.

Movies that Matter: Reading Film Through the Lens of Faith by Richard Leonard, S. J. This book is worth its price just for the fourteen-page introduction. In a very concise way, Leonard teaches us how to *read* a film from a Christian point of view. He then lifts teachable moments found in fifty different movies and provides questions for personal reflection or group dialogue.

Pop Goes Religion: Faith in Popular Culture by Terry Mattingly. Terry is a nationally syndicated journalist who has written articles for years about arts and religion. This book is a compilation of articles he wrote between 1997 and 2005 and covers the convergence of faith and popular culture in six areas: music, movies, TV shows, books, fantasy, and commercials.

Simply Strategic Growth by Tim Stevens and Tony Morgan. Okay, it looks like I'm pimping one of my books again. Yes, I am. But hear me out. This book answers so many of the specific "how to" questions that are asked about leveraging culture. How do you plan services? How do you decide which series to offer? How do you find creative people? How do you promote a series? Tony and I offer ninety-nine strategies for attracting a crowd to your church in short two- or three-page chapters. It's the type of book you can put on the back of your toilet and get through in a few weeks (unless you get sick, and then you might make it in a few days).

Static by Ron Martoia. I'll admit I wasn't too excited about reading this book, that is, until I started reading it. Then I couldn't put it down. Martoia uses an easy-to-read story format and redefines some of the often-used but rarely understood terms in Christianity—words that are confusing to us and distracting to others. This is the one book I am listing that does not directly talk about engaging the culture but is included here for this reason: Many of the verses used to perpetrate an isolationist, stay-as-far-away-from-the-culture-as-you-can type of theology, are really being taken way out of their historical context.

If you are still struggling with, "Well what about such and such a verse that says we should stay away from the culture?"—read Martoia's book.

The Rock Cries Out: Discovering Eternal Truth in Unlikely Music by Steve Stockman. In this book, the author explores the music of twelve artists who have not necessarily professed a Christian faith but whose work is undergirded with issues, questions, and insights that are very much biblical. Stockman profiles George Harrison, Bob Dylan, Bob Marley, Lauryn Hill, and others.

Walk On: The Spiritual Journey of U2 by Steve Stockman. This Presbyterian minister from Ireland seems to know a whole lot about the rock group U2. He documents their history of ups and downs through the years, as well as exposes the real meanings behind many of their songs and performances. Be sure to get the updated and expanded edition published in 2005 by Relevant Books.

What Can Be Found in Lost by John Ankerberg and Dillon Burroughs. Another confession—I love this show! This book explores the spiritual truths in the hit ABC show *Lost*. The authors don't pretend that it is a Christian show but rather suggest it addresses some deep spiritual issues about the existence of God, miracles, the nature of good and evil, the afterlife, redemption, forgiveness, and destiny.

MAGAZINES

Collide—Known as the magazine that highlights "where media and the church converge," this periodical premiered in September 2007. It is published bi-monthly and is a tremendous resource for any church leader who is using media and leveraging the culture. Oh, and it is especially valuable because I write a column in every issue.

KEYWORD: STUFF | PopGoesTheChurch.com

Entertainment Weekly—I read this magazine cover-to-cover every · week. It keeps me up-to-speed on issues and trends in the culture and helps me think ahead about what the culture might be talking about a few months down the road. (We use this in planning weekend series at Granger.)

Relevant—Erwin McManus once said, "If you are talking about being relevant, you aren't." But this magazine is. I'm guessing it is the most widely known magazine that covers topics from faith to life to progressive culture. It is definitely a tool that practices the art of finding truth in the culture—wherever that might be.

Risen—This is a high quality magazine that includes fascinating interviews with mainstream artists in the culture. Their commitment is to explore culture through the prism of faith, transformation, and truth.

WEBSITES 🖥⁾

BestWeekEver.tv—This site is sponsored by VH1, and it gives an overview of pop culture happenings in the news. It is sometimes earthy, often sarcastic, and probably not a site you want to look at with your children in the room. However, I find it valuable for keeping me up on the news, as well as sometimes giving me a glimpse of how pop culture views followers of Christ.

DickStaub.com—The recent author of *The Culturally Savvy Christian*, Dick Staub has a fascination with America's spiritual quest, which today is often unlinked from organized religion. He believes there is a vibrant ongoing conversation about "ideas that matter" and beliefs going on in today's popular culture through movies, books, theater,

🖥⁾ KEYWORD: STUFF | PopGoesTheChurch.com

and music. Part of his mission is to listen to and facilitate that cultural conversation, and he does that well through his website, blog, and newsletter.

HollywoodJesus.com—The site is described as "pop culture from a spiritual point of view." It is primarily a site with reviews by Christians of movies, music, TV shows, books, comics, and games. I'm not crazy about the cluttered design of the website, and I don't always agree with the reviewers' opinions, but I find it a great resource.

LeadingSmart.com—This is the home of my personal blog. My primary focus is helping church leaders around the world be better, smarter leaders. This is where you'll find my freshest thoughts on church, family, culture, leadership, and more.

PopGoesTheChurch.com—The companion website for this book. You have noticed keywords throughout the book, and the purpose of the website is to continue the conversation. The danger of writing a book like this is that it is outdated the day it is published. But the website will be kept full of current content, resources, and links to help you continue to leverage the culture.

PopMatters.com—*PopMatters* is an international online magazine about all things pop culture. It includes intelligent reviews, engaging interviews, and in-depth essays on most cultural products and expressions in areas such as music, television, films, books, video games, sports, theater, the visual arts, travel, and the internet.

Thunderstruck.org—Steve Beard is the creator of this website and is a writer for *Good News Magazine, Risen Magazine,* and *National Review.* I am amazed at how he loads up this website with hundreds of articles and links to stories and sites that feature faith, culture, or the convergence of the two. You will be amazed by how much information Steve is able to find and make available.

VIDEO RESOURCES FOR CHURCHES🖳⁾

Several companies exist to provide churches with material to help reach our video-intensive culture. Here are a few to get you started:

AngelHouseMedia.com
BlueFishTV.com
Eleven72.com
FaithVisuals.com
FortyOneTwenty.com
HighwayVideo.com
IgniterMedia.com
LifeChurch.tv

MidnightOilProductions.com
RadiateFilms.com
SermonSpice.com
SermonVideos.com
WingClips.com
WiredChurches.com
WorshipFilms.com
WorshipHouseMedia.com

POP CULTURE SERIES FROM GRANGER🖳⁾

I realize this list will be immediately outdated, but I include it to illustrate how pop culture can be leveraged to communicate biblical truth. Check out PopGoesTheChurch.com for examples that are more recent.

🖳⁾ KEYWORD: STUFF | PopGoesTheChurch.com

I Love the '80s: Big Hair. Bad Debt. Good Music (February 2008)—Each year we tackle the topic of giving and selfishness, and what better way to do it than through the music and images of the '80s. With music by Madonna and Van Halen, dramas featuring *MacGyver* and the *Valley Girls*, and clips from some of the greatest movies of the '80s, we were able to take a sensitive subject (money) and make it fun.

Let It Be Christmas: A Story Told by Matthew, Mark, Luke, John, Paul, George, and Ringo (December 2007)—Each week was titled with a different song from the Beatles. We began with the longings of the Beatles evident in their lyrics and addressed the spiritual issues from the Bible.

Heroes (October 2007)—This series began in the same week the second season of this popular show debuted on NBC. "Have you ever had the feeling you were meant for something extraordinary?" was the theme of the TV show and allowed us to talk about discovering your purpose and making a difference in someone else's life.

The Office (September 2007)—Using clips from the popular TV show, along with some original dramas based on the hit, this series addressed the issues we all face in our jobs. Topics included ethics in the workplace, balance of priorities, and dealing with difficult people. Billboards went up all over town for this series with an encouragement to visit MyOfficeSecrets.com to confess your workplace shenanigans.

Deal or No Deal (June 2007)—This was a three-week series that launched with a humorous drama based on the popular TV game show. Each week tackled a different topic about money and demonstrated how our values are upside down to God's values.

The Enemy Within (May 2007)—Launched to coincide with the release of *Spider-Man 3: The Enemy Within*, we tackled the five main topics from the movie: temptation, bitterness, selfishness, insecurity, and gossip.

Sound Vows (April 2007)—This was a series on marriage, and each message was the title of a current Top 40 song. "The Lips of an Angel" (Hinder) was a week on guarding your marriage. "Feel the Silence" (Goo Goo Dolls) was about communication, and "She's Everything" (Brad Paisley) was about making intentional choices to honor your spouse.

24. Your Time. Your Choice (January 2007)—In order to leverage the marketing of the TV show, we timed our series with the beginning of a new season. In this series of messages, we considered what it would be like if you integrated your faith into your life 24/7. What if you looked at every area of your life through God's eyes, instead of adding God to your schedule one time each week?

When Love Comes to Town: A U2 Christmas (December 2006)—One of our highest attended series ever, we took the songs of U2 and interviews with Bono, and again considered what the Bible had to say about the questions and spiritual issues raised in their music.

Reel Dating (September 2006)—A series to help couples in love using movie titles (and clips) to focus on the topic. *Hitch* was about commitment. *Meet the Parents* offered help for parents as they prepare their younger children for relationships. *Mr. and Mrs. Smith* encouraged married couples never to stop dating.

Click (June 2006)—The start of this series coincided with the launch of the Adam Sandler movie. It did not have anything to do with the content of the movie, but we just used the concept (and the image of a remote control) to build a message around each of our five focus areas for the year.

Face the Music: Finding God in your iPod (May 2006)—This was another series that capitalized on current hit songs. "iSearch" was all about leveraging today's music to have spiritual conversations and featured "Savin' Me" (Nickelback). Another week, called "iRest," encouraged everyone to slow down and focus on what is important, using "Living in Fast Forward" (Kenny Chesney) to help communicate.

Unlocking the DaVinci Code: Living the Mystery (April 2006)—As you may recall, there were tons of media focus and religious fervor surrounding this movie. We capitalized on that and intentionally talked about some of the big issues from the book upon which the movie was based, including the mystery of Jesus, the mystery of the arts, and the mystery of the Bible.

CONFERENCES

Here are a few conferences that either are focused on leveraging the culture or are sponsored by churches that do a good job at it.

Catalyst (CatalystConference.com)—If you want to get fired up, join ten thousand other young church leaders for this two-day event held yearly north of Atlanta, Georgia.

Creative Church Conference (CreativePastors.com)—From Ed Young Jr. and the team at Fellowship Church in Grapevine, Texas. I have been several times and have always loved it.

Drive (DriveConference.com)—From Andy Stanley and the team at North Point Community Church in Alpharetta, Georgia. This church has it going on.

Innovate (WiredChurches.com)—If you only attend one conference, go to this one. I'm slightly biased since Granger hosts it, but I think I would tell you that even if I moved away.

Innovative Impact (i2conference.com)—From Kerry Shook and his team at Fellowship of the Woodlands in Houston, Texas.

KEYWORD: STUFF | PopGoesTheChurch.com

Q (FermiProject.com/q)—A bit pricey, but Q is a place where innovators, church leaders, social entrepreneurs, and cultural leaders come together to explore the church's role in positively contributing to culture.

Unleash (NewSpringOnline.com)—From world-class blogger Perry Noble and team, this is the only one-day conference in the mix. I haven't been but have heard it is great.

Willow Creek Arts Conference (WillowCreek.com)—Anyone who says this church is no longer on the cutting-edge hasn't visited lately. I was pleasantly surprised when I attended this conference in June 2007.

POP GOES THE CHURCH—THE WORKSHOP

Several times each year, we offer an interactive one-day workshop for leaders who want to drill down even more on this topic. Not only do I teach portions of this book, but also give practical examples, show video clips, and engage the audience with answers to their specific ministry questions. This workshop is offered a couple times each year in Granger (and who wouldn't want to visit the upper Midwest?) as well as in cities around the United States. See WiredChurches.com for more information.

⌨)) KEYWORDS

ENDNOTES

INTRODUCTION P.13

1. Impact. Dictionary.com. *The American Heritage® Dictionary of the English Language, Fourth Edition*. Houghton Mifflin Company, 2004. http://dictionary.reference.com/browse/impact (accessed: January 29, 2008).

2. Eugene H. Peterson, *The Message: The Bible in Contemporary Language* (NavPress Publishing Group, 2002).

3. See Mark 7:1–20.

CHAPTER 1: "MOLLY, YOUR CHURCH SUCKS!" P.23

Epigraph: D. Elton Trueblood, as quoted by Terry Mattingly, *Pop Goes Religion* (Nashville, TN: W Publishing Group, 2005), 68.

1. Bono in a video interview by Bill Hybels as presented at the Leadership Summit, August 2006.

2. David Kinnaman and Gabe Lyons, *unChristian* (Grand Rapids, MI: Baker Books, 2007), 29–30.

3. David Kinnaman and Gabe Lyons, *unChristian* (Grand Rapids, MI: Baker Books, 2007), 122.

4. G. Jeffery MacDonald, "More Americans' Spiritual Life Nurtured Within," *USA Today*, January 13, 2008.

5. George Barna writing the foreword for Jim Henderson and Matt Casper, *Jim & Casper Go to Church* (Carol Stream, IL: BarnaBooks, 2007), x.

6. See http://www.leadingsmart.com/leadingsmart/2007/08/willow-teach-pe.html

7. Rick Warren, *The Purpose-Driven Church* (Grand Rapids, MI: Zondervan Publishing House, 1995), 49.

8. George Barna, *The Barna Update*, February 2001. See http://www.barna.org/FlexPage.aspx?Page=BarnaUpdate&BarnaUpdateID=81

9. David Kinnaman and Gabe Lyons, *unChristian* (Grand Rapids, MI: Baker Books, 2007), 130.

10. See Genesis 1:27.

11. Coldplay, "Fix You," *X & Y*, Capitol Records, 2005.

12. Craig Detweiler and Barry Taylor, *A Matrix of Meanings* (Grand Rapids, MI: Baker Academic, 2005), 9.

13. George Barna, *Revolution* (Carol Stream, IL: BarnaBooks, 2005), 31.

14. George Barna, *Revolution* (Carol Stream, IL: BarnaBooks, 2005), 39.

CHAPTER 2: LOST IN TRANSLATION P.41

1. See http://www.brandchannel.com/start1.asp?fa_id=340

2. Chip Heath and Dan Heath, *Made to Stick* (New York, NY: Random House, 2007), 20.

3. Ron Martoia, *Static* (Carol Stream, IL: Tyndale House Publishers, 2007), 12. Used by permission.

4. Julia Reed, "A Campus Culture Which Spurns the Misfits," *Sunday Telegraph*, April 25, 1999, 31.

CHAPTER 3: WHY POP CULTURE IS SO POPULAR P.53

Epigraph: George Barna and Mark Hatch, *Boiling Point* (Ventura, CA: Regal Books, 2003), 188.

1. Craig Detweiler and Barry Taylor, *A Matrix of Meanings* (Grand Rapids, MI: Baker Academic, 2003), 18.

2. Information from the National Cable & Telecommunications Association, http://www.ncta.com/ContentView.aspx?contentId=2685

3. *USA Today*, September 21, 2006, http://www.usatoday.com/life/television/news/2006-09-21-homes-tv_x.htm

4. Norman Herr, Ph.D., Professor of Science Education, California State University, http://www.csun.edu/science/health/docs/tv&health.html

5. According to Nielsen NetRatings, August 2007, http://www.nielsen-netratings.com

6. According to the Recording Industry Association of America, www.riaa.com.

7. According to the Motion Picture Association release of *2006 U.S. Theatrical Market Statistics*.

8. Walter Kirn, *Here, There and Everywhere,* February 11, 2007 edition of *New York Times Magazine*.

9. David Kinnaman and Gabe Lyons, *unChristian* (Grand Rapids, MI: Baker-Books, 2007), 11.

10. George Barna writing the foreword for Jim Henderson and Matt Casper, *Jim & Casper Go to Church* (Carol Stream, IL: BarnaBooks, 2007), xi.

11. Terry Mattingly, *Pop Goes Religion* (Nashville, TN: W Publishing Group, 2005), xxi.

12. Terry Mattingly, *Pop Goes Religion* (Nashville, TN: W Publishing Group, 2005), xx.

13. Richard Leonard, *Movies that Matter* (Chicago, IL: Loyola Press, 2006), xi.

14. David Kinnaman and Gabe Lyons, *unChristian* (Grand Rapids, MI: Barna-Books, 2007), 23.

15. Craig Detweiler and Barry Taylor, *A Matrix of Meanings* (Grand Rapids, MI: Baker Academic, 2003), 10.

16. *Parade Magazine,* October 7, 2007, http://www.parade.com/articles/editions/2007/edition_10-07-2007/Brad_Pitt

17. William D. Romanowski, *Eyes Wide Open* (Brazos, A Division of Baker Publishing Group, 2007), 76. Used by permission.

CHAPTER 4: A TALE OF FIVE CHURCHES P.65

1. David Kinnaman and Gabe Lyons, *unChristian* (Grand Rapids, MI: Baker Books, 2007), p. 26.

2. Craig Detweiler and Barry Taylor, *A Matrix of Meanings* (Grand Rapids, MI: Baker Academic, 2003), 10.

3. David Kinnaman and Gabe Lyons, *unChristian* (Grand Rapids, MI: Baker Books, 2007), 181.

4. Matthew 12:1-6 by Eugene H. Peterson in *The Message: The Bible in Contemporary*

Language (NavPress Publishing Group, 2002).

5. Matthew 12:34.

6. Steven Furtick, *All About the Numbers*, Aug 21, 2007, http://www.stevenfurtick.com/elevation/all-about-the-numbers/

7. *Outreach Magazine*, http://www.outreachmagazine.com/library/features/documents/thelist1.pdf

8. Craig Groeschel, Pastor of LifeChurch.tv, as published on Swerve, *Future of the Church Part 2 of 5*, http://swerve.lifechurch.tv/2007/10/16/future-of-the-church-2-of-5/

CHAPTER 5: LINKIN PARK SINGS. GOD SPEAKS. P.83

Epigraph: John Calvin, as quoted by William D. Romanowski, *Eyes Wide Open* (Brazos, A Division of Baker Publishing Group, 2007), 89. Used by permission.

1. According to Wikipedia, http://en.wikipedia.org/wiki/Google_Book_Search

2. See http://en.wikipedia.org/wiki/List_of_music_genres

3. Acts 17:22–23.

4. Steve Stockman, *The Rock Cries Out* (Lake Mary, FL: Relevant Books, 2004), 4.

5. Luke 19:40, Today's New International Version.

6. Steve Stockman, *The Rock Cries Out* (Lake Mary, FL: Relevant Books, 2004), p. 2.

7. Linkin Park, "Numb," *Meteora*, Warner Bros., 2003.

8. Jeremiah 45:3, paraphrased by Eugene H. Peterson in *The Message: The Bible in Contemporary Language* (NavPress Publishing Group, 2002).

9. Linkin Park, "Easier to Run," *Meteora*, Warner Bros., 2003.

10. Desperate Housewives, *Smiles of a Summer Night*, Season 4, Episode 2, first aired 10/7/2007.

11. Craig Detweiler and Barry Taylor, *A Matrix of Meanings* (Grand Rapids, MI: Baker Academic, 2003), 11.

12. Madeleine L'Engle, *Walking on Water* (Chicago, IL: Shaw Books, 2001), 46.

13. Steve Stockman, *Walk on: The Spiritual Journey of U2* (Lake Mary, FL: Relevant Books, 2005), xiii.

14. Craig Detweiler and Barry Taylor, *A Matrix of Meanings* (Grand Rapids, MI: Baker Academic, 2003), 8.

CHAPTER 6: FINDING GOD IN POP CULTURE IS EASIER THAN YOU THINK P.95

Epigraph: Richard Leonard, *Movies That Matter* (Chicago, IL: Loyola Press, 2006), xii.

1. Craig Detweiler and Barry Taylor, *A Matrix of Meanings* (Grand Rapids, MI: Baker Academic, 2003), 318.

2. Romans 8:23, by Eugene H. Peterson in *The Message: The Bible in Contemporary Language* (NavPress Publishing Group, 2002).

3. TVGuide.com, *Holly Hunter: Saving Grace is Very Risky Business*, July 23, 2007, http://www.tvguide.com/news/holly-hunter-grace/070723-02

4. Matthew 22:37–39.

5. *Friday Night Lights*, NBC, *Let's Get It On*, Episode #205, first aired November 2, 2007.

6. Terry Mattingly, *Pop Goes Religion* (Nashville, TN: W Publishing Group, 2005), 104.

7. Colossians 1:16, by Eugene H. Peterson in *The Message: The Bible in Contemporary Language* (NavPress Publishing Group, 2002).

8. Romans 12:19.

9. *Entertainment Weekly*, Sep 14, 2007, 59.

10. Gareth Higgins, *How Movies Helped Save My Soul* (Lake Mary, FL: Relevant Books, 2004), x.

CHAPTER 7: SCRATCH PEOPLE WHERE THEY ITCH P.109

1. Terry Mattingly, *Pop Goes Religion* (Nashville, TN: W Publishing Group, 2005), 30.

CHAPTER 8: I'M NOT A THEOLOGIAN, BUT... P.123

1. 2 Timothy 4:3.

2. Quoted directly from a video recording of the service.

3. According to the Archaeological Study Bible, *The Areopagus* (Grand Rapids, MI: Zondervan, 2005), 1802. This stairway "is still used today, although centuries of wear have left the steps extremely slippery."

4. Acts 17:22–23, by Eugene H. Peterson in *The Message: The Bible in Contemporary Language* (NavPress Publishing Group, 2002).

5. Titus 1:12, by Eugene H. Peterson in *The Message: The Bible in Contemporary Language* (NavPress Publishing Group, 2002).

6. 1 Corinthians 15:33.

7. According to the Archaeological Study Bible, *Introduction to Proverbs* (Grand Rapids, MI: Zondervan, 2005), 958.

8. According to the Archaeological Study Bible (Grand Rapids, MI: Zondervan, 2005), 1010, Proverbs 31:10–31 are written in an acrostic with each verse beginning with a successive letter of the Hebrew alphabet.

9. Madeleine I. Boucher, *Parables* (Michael Glazier, 1981), as quoted on PBS.org, "From Jesus to Christ," http://www.pbs.org/wgbh/pages/frontline/shows/religion/jesus/parables.html

10. Leland Ryken, *Words of Delight* (Grand Rapids, MI: Baker Academic, 1992), 405.

11. Richard Leonard, *Movies that Matter* (Chicago, IL: Loyola Press, 2006), xvii.

12. 2 Timothy 4:3.

13. Rick Warren, *The Purpose-Driven Church* (Grand Rapids, MI: Zondervan Publishing House, 1995), 219.

14. Richard Leonard, *Movies that Matter* (Chicago, IL: Loyola Press, 2006), xvii.

15. Luke 13:1–4.

16. John 17:15.

17. Tom Wright, *John for Everyone: Part Two* (Louisville, KY: Westminster John Knox Press, 2004), 95.

18. Matthew 11:18–19.

19. John 4:5–29.

20. Luke 7:36–50.

21. 1 Corinthians 9:19–22.

22. Romans 12:1–2, by Eugene H. Peterson in *The Message: The Bible in Contemporary Language* (NavPress Publishing Group, 2002).

CHAPTER 9: CREATE A LITTLE BUZZ P.137

1. See http://youtube.com/watch?v=hMnk7lh9M3o

2. According to IMDB.com trivia, http://www.imdb.com/title/tt0185937/trivia

3. Mark Hughes, *Buzzmarketing* (New York, NY: Penguin Group, 2005), 38.

4. Emanuel Rosen, *The Anatomy of Buzz: How to Create Word of Mouth Marketing* (New York, NY: Currency Business Books, 2002).

5. South Bend Tribune, *What's With Those Feet? Here's The Scoop,* March 2, 2006, p. A1.

CHAPTER 10: THE BEATLES AND DESPERATE HOUSEWIVES GO TO CHURCH P.147

1. See chapter 5 for a discussion on "secular" vs. "sacred" music.

2. Acts 17:28. See chapter 8 on theology for more.

3. These three components have been in play at Granger for many years. Tony Morgan first wrote about this strategy in January 2006 at Pastors.com: http://www.pastors.com/RWMT/?ID=241&artid=9025&expand=1

4. John 1:14, by Eugene H. Peterson in *The Message: The Bible in Contemporary Language* (NavPress Publishing Group, 2002).

CHAPTER 11: LET'S GET IT STARTED P.159

1. Hebrews 13:17, by Eugene H. Peterson in *The Message: The Bible in Contemporary Language* (NavPress Publishing Group, 2002).

2. 1 Corinthians 5:12–13.

3. According to *Outreach Magazine*, January 2007 and January 2008.

4. See http://www.copyright.gov/fls/fl102.html

CHAPTER 12: TWENTY CHURCHES. TWENTY STORIES. P.177

1. Os Guiness, *Prophetic Untimeliness: A Challenge to the Idol of Relevance* (Grand Rapids, MI: Baker Books, 2005).

CHAPTER 13: SO THAT... P.221

1. James 1:22-25.

TIM STEVENS

Follower of Jesus. It's what guides his passion to ask questions and learn something from everyone. He never gets tired of it—dreaming and coloring outside the lines— always looking for a new way to communicate God's truth.

Husband devoted to Faith, the woman who still gets his motor running after twenty years like she did the first time he saw her getting off the church bus in 1988. She complements his strengths and fills the gap.

Father to four children in three different schools. Heather, Megan, Hunter, and Taylor keep him running between high school, middle school, elementary school, cross-country, choir, band, soccer, Awana, the Apple Store—well, you get the idea.

Pastor on Granger Community Church's (GCCwired.com) executive leadership team since 1994, successfully blending innovative outreach and disciple-ship, helping thousands take their next step towards Christ. He is responsible for a staff of ninety-plus change agents that serve not only the local community but also hundreds of church plants throughout India.

Author of the *Simply Strategic* book series with Tony Morgan. But, he doesn't stop there. Tim blogs about specific and practical resources at PopGoestheChurch.com and LeadingSmart.com to equip and encourage church leaders in an ongoing conversation.

Designer of weekend service experiences and church buildings that help create the space for people to meet God. In his free time, he keeps it going with sheds, home additions, and renovations. Carpentry and artistry are in his blood.

Strategist who takes big vision and translates it into simple tools that help bring out the best in people and teams so they can soar.

Geek an enthusiastic fan of technology, gadgets, and basically anything that plugs in. Is it to a sometimes excessive degree? Nah, he still does his research and uses it to connect with people. 💻

💻 KEYWORD: TIM | PopGoesTheChurch.com

MY REVIEW TEAM

I am incredibly grateful for the team of men and women who spent hours reviewing the manuscript and offering suggestions to make it better. Their input was candid, refreshing, enlightening, thoughtful, and unbelievably helpful. *Pop Goes the Church* is better because of their time.

Bob Adams, Waupaca, WI

Dave Anderson, Decatur, AL

Greg Baird, Jamul, CA

Dawn Nicole Baldwin, Sycamore, IL

Rich Barrett, Jacksonville, FL

Dennis Bauer, Richland, MI

Mark Beeson, Granger, IN

Rob Bergman, St. Louis, MO

Reg Bertrand, Ontario, Canada

Brian Blough, Granger, IN

Larry Boatright, Sherman, TX

Steven Bruce, Amarillo, TX

Steve Caronna, Raleigh, NC

Barrett Case, Overbrook, KS

Julie Chaisson, Nova Scotia, Canada

Andrew Conard, Leawood, KS

Evan Courtney, Mattoon, IL

Amber Cox, Grand Rapids, MI

Tim Cox, Miamisburg, OH

Terrace Crawford, Norfolk, VA

Robert Culler, Frostburg, MD

DC Curry, Granger, IN

Craig Dale, Galt, CA

Michael Danner, Metamora, IL

Dave Davis, Richmond, TX

Trevor Davis, Chula Vista, CA

Jerry Day, Columbus, IN

Lisa DeSelm, South Bend, IN

Ryan DeVries, Chennai, India

Johnny Douglas, Brentwood, England

Ben Dubow, Storrs, CT

Tim Dunn, Cincinnati, OH

Seleta Edge, Sulphur Springs, TX

Rob Edwards, Portsmouth, VA

Blair Farley, Irvine, CA

Aaron Floyd, Pocatello, ID

Milan Ford, Conyers, GA

Lorin Foster, Warren, OH

Gordon Franklin, Heath, OH

Chris Freeland, Fort Worth, TX

Jack Fussell, Morocco

Jeff Geshay, Newark, DE

Steven Gibbs, Alpharetta, GA

Craig Gorc, Bothell, WA

Lary Gray, Norman, OK

Michael Head, Houston, TX

Jim Henry, Bloomington, IL

Jerrod Hoeft, Granger, IN

Theresa Hoeft, Granger, IN

Wes Humble, Newark, OH

Luke Humbrecht, Longmont, CO

Lee Insko, Georgetown, KY

Jeremy Isaacs, Marietta, GA

Jeremy Johnson, Murfreesboro, TN

Terry Johnson, Wichita, KS

Keith Jones, Queen Creek, AZ

Shane Kennard, Heber Springs, AR

Matt Kerner, Springfield, MO

Dan Kyles, Dunedin, New Zealand

Mike Laurence, Hopkinton, MA

Michael Lukaszewski, Cartersville, GA

Scott Magdalein, Jacksonville, FL

Kendra Malloy, Troy, MI

Corey Mann, Granger, IN

Jeremy Marshall, Summerville, GA

Doug Mathers, Rochester, MN

Willy Maxwell, Riverton, WY

Chad McCallum, Byron Center, MI

Trey McClain, Evansville, IN

Clif McKinley, Rochester, NH

Kem Meyer, Granger, IN

Mark Meyer, Granger, IN

Ross Middleton, Tallahassee, FL

Jason Miller, South Bend, IN

Zach Montroy, Aurora, IL

Rebecca Moon, Loganville, GA

Brett Morey, Acworth, GA

Tony Morgan, Anderson, SC

Beth Nelson, Atlanta, GA

James Owolabi, Belfair, WA

Kevin D. Osborn, Wichita, KS

Scott Palmer, Rochester, MN

Steve Patton, Newport, RI

Cole Phillips, Kyle, TX

Scott Pusey, Bigler, PA

Jeff Reed, Miami, FL

Keith Rhodes, Haughton, LA

Andrew Romstad, Cambridge, MN

Trace Rorie, South Bend, IN

Kenneth C. Row, Dayton, IN

Jami Ruth, South Bend, IN

Jason Salamun, Rapid City, SD

Eric Sanderson, Oklahoma City, OK

Dale Schaeffer, Morton, IL

Tim Schraeder, Chicago, IL

Daniel Scott, Grand Rapids, MI

Matt Singley, Los Angeles, CA

Doug Smith, Huntersville, NC

Greg Smith, Wichita, KS

Marcy Smith, Huntsersville, NC

Taylor Smith, Alexandria, LA

John Stark, Des Moines, IA

Isaiah Surbrook, Wilmore, KY

Louis Tagliaboschi, Bowling Green, KY

Travis Thompson, Winter Haven, FL

Gilbert Thurston, Chambersburg, PA

Sam Todd, Ponca, NE

David Turner, Plainfield, IL

Julie Turner, Granger, IN

Mark Turner, Granger, IN

Kim Volheim, Granger, IN

Dan Vukmirovich, South Bend, IN

Steven Wales, Nazareth, PA

Mark Waltz, Mishawaka, IN

Aaron Warner, Altoona, IA

Jesse Watson, Surprise, AZ

Rob Wegner, Granger, IN

Butch Whitmire, Granger, IN

Carlos Whittaker, Atlanta, GA

Joe Wickman, Binghamton, NY

Shawn Wood, Mount Pleasant, SC

Matthew Zook, Mishawaka, IN

NOTES

NOTES

NOTES